C000181142

How to create a co
to grow your

Recruit,

 Inspire

& Retain

JACQUI MANN

R3THINK PRESS

First published in Great Britain 2018
by Rethink Press (www.rethinkpress.com)

Praise

'Jacqui Mann's passion for creating a great place to work is clear. An informative book for people interested in developing their culture.'

GEORGINA EL MORSHDY
Owner, Gem Writing

'I thought I understood this subject but I have been introduced to some very interesting ideas.'

CLIVE BINGHAM
Owner, CAB Consulting

'It's as if Jacqui has captured the good, bad and ugly from my experiences of twenty-five years in corporate life. This is a must-read for anyone running a business – however small or large the team. With practical exercises and real-life examples from some of the world's leading companies on culture, this book is certainly not fluffy.'

JACKI NORBURY
Marketing Director, Advocate Business Services

Contents

To my family

'Without you nothing else has a purpose'
I love you all more than you will ever know

Foreword

'When people say to me: would you rather be thought of as a funny man or a great boss? My answer's always the same: to me, they're not mutually exclusive.'

This was one of the most cringe-inducing lines ever delivered by David Brent during the first episode of BBC's *The Office*, a documentary-style sitcom following the goings-on at a suburban paper company where life is stationary. Brent, played by Ricky Gervais, is a white-collar office middle manager and the principal character of the series, which centres on his many idiosyncrasies, hypocrisies, self-delusions and overt self-promotion.

Of course, Brent's character is exaggerated, but the reason the show is so cringe-worthy is because as the audience, we know deep down that we've come across someone like this in our real-life work place. And worse, many viewers would have had experiences of how not to manage people, or indeed a business (I know I certainly have a boxful of examples from my working life). Even Gervais himself revealed that his character, Brent, was actually based on a number of people he'd met during the time that he'd spent working in offices in his earlier years.

But while *The Office* was comical, the real issues it brought to life weren't.

I wasn't remotely surprised when Jacqui told me about her book. I've known Jacqui for seven years and in that time I've heard her speak on stage to large audiences, challenge others and share honest feedback in Masterminds, and I was fortunate to be her mentor/coach for a period of time to help scale her own business. (I quickly learnt that Jacqui was an expert in her field of HR and people, so she didn't need any help with that! As Jacqui explains in Chapter 10: 'If you don't have a coach you're seriously undermining your potential.')

I run a mentoring business for owners who are serious about growth, and our programs are all based around my Scale Model™ and philosophy. Unlike many other coaches/mentors or programmes, the first thing we focus on with a new client is not their strategy – it's their environment. One of my mentors, Daniel Priestley, once said to me, 'Your business environment will dictate your performance.' By reading this book, you will understand what is meant by environment, and you'll go through a step-by-step practical guide on how to get the right set-up for your business. Even if you've been operating for more than ten years, it's not too late. If you can't provide the necessary resources, build a culture and make decisions, then you're never going to deliver the performance.

One of the questions I get asked most frequently is, 'How do I get my staff to care as much as I do? Why don't they get it?' And this is exactly the question Jacqui addresses and answers throughout *Recruit, Inspire & Retain* – and with real honesty, because she understands your frustrations as she's been on both sides of the wall. What makes her advice so unique is her ability to bring corporate thinking to the SME world (the good, the bad and the ugly), as well as real-life examples from successful companies such as Infusionsoft and Zappos. These aren't quotes you can get off the internet, these are the result of one-to-one interviews as part of Jacqui's research. Some great lessons for us all to learn.

Finally, it's important for you to understand that some people will help you reach your goals, and others will hold you back. Some people have no aspiration to start a business, grow it and then free themselves from the day-to-day. If you are reading this book, then you are not one of those people. And you have chosen well: to focus on your people and on creating your own culture.

So I hope you will join me in Jacqui's call to arms in creating an entrepreneur's cultural revolution.

MARTIN NORBURY
The Scalability Coach and author of *I Don't Work Fridays*

Introduction

If I had a penny for every time a business owner told me they had a problem with a member of staff, I would be a millionaire by now. Employing people can be stressful, complicated and frustrating (I know, I'm a business owner too), and as the business owner you think no one understands or cares about the business as you do. Business owners can struggle with the growing pains of their business and most of the time people are the cause of these pains. You are working hard to make your business successful, but for some reason the staff don't seem to be interested. You struggle to recruit the right people, staff make mistakes – they are just not motivated.

For a business to grow, be successful and profitable, the staff need to be on board, engaged, inspired and understand why they come to work every day. More importantly, they should want to come to work every day and feel valued. You understand if you want your business to grow you need to do something about it, but you're not sure what or even how to cure the people problems. Unfortunately there is not a pill you can take to make everything better.

Recruit, Inspire & Retain is for business owners who employ 6–200 staff, who want to scale or exit their business and want to find a cure for their people problems. The book's focus is on how to create a company culture, which is now recognised as a must-have rather than a nice-to-have. Some of the most successful brands in the world – Virgin, Google, Zappos, Starbucks, Infusionsoft and Disney – have amazingly strong company cultures. They understood the importance of culture as they grew, even before they became hugely successful. A great culture creates a positive workplace with engaged employees. Investing in your company culture shows your employees that you care and makes them feel valued. A great workplace culture doesn't happen by accident. Instead, it's created purposefully.

Establishing a culture is not just something large corporate businesses do. Every business can define the culture they want. I am going to share with you what I have learnt over the years. I want you to understand that you, too, can do this in your business; you don't have to be Google, Facebook or Starbucks to do it. I promise that if you create a positive culture your business will be transformed.

As part of my research for this book I was fortunate enough to be able to interview Kelly Wolske, a trainer at Zappos, and Dan Ralphs, the 'dream manager' at Infusionsoft. Both of these companies have amazing cultures and some great lessons can be learnt from them. I will share with you some of the insights and ideas from these companies.

This book will guide you through the steps you need to take to create a company culture that has a purpose. I worked in corporates for many years and I want to share my knowledge with you, to give you the opportunity to define your culture. I will share ideas of how some large companies have embedded their culture. This will enable you to take some of those ideas and make them relevant to your business. A strong culture will ensure your business has a life beyond you. It will strengthen your business brand and, more importantly, attract, inspire and retain the right staff, which in turn will cure your people problems.

About me

I am the founder and managing director of J Mann Associates, and I am known as the P.E.O.P.L.E.™ Doctor. As an HR expert, I specialise in creating great places to work. Since founding my HR outsourcing business in 2003, I have been supporting entrepreneurial business owners across the UK who are looking to scale or exit their business. As well as providing support through the People Foundations for these businesses, I work on consultancy projects, and my specialist area is in company culture and change management.

I've worked with large corporates and hundreds of entrepreneurial business owners in various industries, including hospitality, retail, care homes, day nurseries, manufacturing, service sectors, and construction. I have a background in executive coaching, HR and business, and I've been studying the wide-reaching impact people make on an organisation for over twenty years.

During my time working at a large corporate I began to understand the importance of creating a great workplace culture. Staff who don't see where their role fits in the bigger picture can cause problems, make mistakes, and lead you to believe that they don't care about the business. Demotivated staff can cause big problems and it can spread like a virus through the business. This can lead to a toxic culture. The company I worked for only paid lip service to the culture and the values. This had a huge effect on me, I became so unhappy I didn't want to go to work. I personally understand what it feels like to work in a company where the culture and values are not lived.

After this experience I was determined to help business owners create a culture that everyone could truly buy into, which in turn has a massive impact on the performance of the business. More importantly, it helps employees find purpose in their work. The magic happens when highly motivated staff work towards a shared purpose and excel in the right role. As a result, even the smallest team can smash targets, innovate and achieve amazing things.

How to use this book

In *Recruit, Inspire & Retain* I outline the six steps in my P.E.O.P.L.E.™ System. I discuss this in detail in Chapter One. The P.E.O.P.L.E.™ System shows how you can embed into your business the mindset and systems necessary to create a great place to work and a culture of purpose. You will discover the techniques to overcome and cure your staff problems, and learn the process I use with my clients to create a great place to work and a culture based on company purpose.

In Chapter Two I examine culture, the impact it has on your business and why you need to focus on it now. Ignoring your culture can be a recipe for disaster.

In Chapter Three I outline the People Foundations that every business needs; after all, you wouldn't start to build a house without first laying the foundations. The foundations are the fundamental building blocks that every business needs in place to ensure they have a solid start to scaling their business.

In Chapters Four to Nine I share the individual steps in my P.E.O.P.L.E.™ System. At the end of each chapter I list the key action steps so you can start implementing the system in your business.

I highly recommend you read the whole book first to give you an understanding of the P.E.O.P.L.E.™ System. I know business owners are busy and want to take action quickly, so if that's you I recommend you read Chapters One to Four first. Don't skip these chapters as they are critical; they underpin everything that creates a great place to work and a strong culture. The other steps in the system are important, but the chapters you choose to read next will depend on the areas you need to work on as a priority. This proven system will transform your business and make your culture a business asset so you can recruit, inspire and retain the right people.

To help you identify your priorities you can download my P.E.O.P.L.E.™ wheel and some other free resources at www.jacquimann.com/resources.

Culture underpins everything in your business. I want every business owner to wake up and understand the massive impact that culture can make on their business. I want you to take that step towards creating a great place to work and creating a culture of purpose.

I want to create an entrepreneur's cultural revolution. The question I ask you is, will you join me? If you want to join me, let's start.

CHAPTER ONE

Does Your Business Have People Disease?

I f you are looking to scale or grow your business then it's more than likely that you will not be able to do this on your own. Most businesses will need to employ people to get the growth they want for their business and to reach their goals. There are not many businesses that don't need to employ people to do this.

If you're struggling to grow your business and achieve your goals because you can't get the right staff, then you've got people problems. It's what I call 'People Disease'.

The symptoms of People Disease vary, but include the following:

- Attitude problems
- Not following processes and procedures

- Employees not caring about the company as you do

- Resistance to change

- Sickness absence

- Lack of passion and commitment

- Does the job that needs to be done and no more

- High staff turnover

- Performance is OK, but nothing to get excited about

Any of these sound familiar?

The three main problems

I've worked with hundreds of business owners during my years in HR and the majority of the businesses have People Disease. I wanted to identify the main problems they were having with their people and find a cure for this disease.

I carried out a survey of business owners and identified the three main problems.

1. You struggle to recruit the right people

2. Employees don't do things the way you want them done

3. Employees don't have the same passion for the business as you do

Let's take a look at each problem in more detail and the issues they cause for the business and you.

You struggle to recruit the right people

Finding the right people can be a long process. When you need someone in the business right now it's sometimes easier to employ someone rather than not have anyone. But is it really? No it isn't. This is the wrong mindset. Recruiting the wrong people is costly for many reasons. Consider how much time you spend on recruitment and training. Then consider the time it takes to remove them from the business if they don't work out. And what about the time it takes to repair any damage they might have caused with customers? Time is money, it all has a cost. What effect does this have on the team when the wrong person is recruited? What damage does that do?

To make matters worse, you need to start the recruitment process all over again.

Without the right people in the business you end up trying to do everything yourself.

Employees don't do things the way you want them done

As the business owner it's frustrating and takes up your valuable time putting things right. When there are four or five employees it is OK, but when you employ more people this can lead to more mistakes and potentially unhappy customers. You then have to spend a huge amount of your time dealing with an employee's poor performance, which can be stressful. Or even worse, you don't deal with the issues and continue to do everything yourself. You are then paying someone and you are still doing the work. Does this sound familiar?

I know as business owners we often think that no one else can do the job as well as us, but do you *know* there are people who can do the job better than you?

Employees don't have the same passion for the business as you

You feel frustrated when employees don't care about the business as you do. They don't have the same motivation as you. You've got some good people but what you really need is a team of engaged, highly motivated individuals who you can rely on, working as a team; employees who will go that extra mile, without being asked; who share your passion for the business. Employees who want to work in your business and help with the growth.

So, put another way, how can you recruit, inspire and retain the right people?

The good news is there is a cure to this People Disease. It's called 'Culture'.

The P.E.O.P.L.E.™ System

Culture is easier to say than to do. Working with my clients I identified the key areas that they needed to address to create and define a great workplace culture. I realised very early on that to attract the right people – and to inspire and retain them in the business – there were some key factors that needed to be included. Once I had identified these I developed the P.E.O.P.L.E.™ System.

The P.E.O.P.L.E.™ System begins with the foundations. It ensures that you have the right foundations in place so employees understand how things are done. It introduces people processes and systems, which will transform your business. I'll cover more of this in Chapter Three.

Once the foundations are laid, it's time to look at the six steps in the P.E.O.P.L.E.™ System. Each of these steps must be in place to create a culture and a great place to work.

The P.E.O.P.L.E.™ System

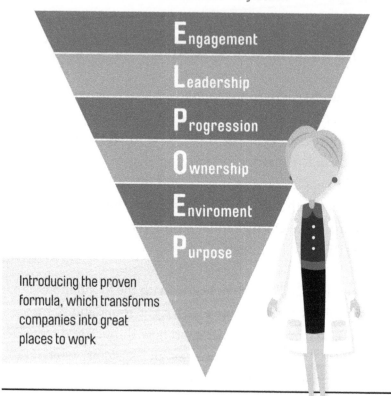

Engagement

Leadership

Progression

Ownership

Enviroment

Purpose

Introducing the proven formula, which transforms companies into great places to work

Foundations

STEP 1: PURPOSE. Your purpose along with your values translates into your culture. What is your company purpose? Is your company purpose clearly defined?

STEP 2: ENVIRONMENT. How does it feel to work in your business? Is it a great place to work?

STEP 3: OWNERSHIP. When staff take ownership, motivation and performance increases. How can you make this happen? Does this happen in your business?

STEP 4: PROGRESSION. Most employees are not motivated by money. How can they progress and develop in your business?

STEP 5: LEADERSHIP. As the leader you need to be the role model of the culture you want to create in your business. Do you walk the talk?

STEP 6: ENGAGEMENT. What is engagement and how do you create it? When does your culture become a business asset?

Before we dive into the People Foundations let's find out in the next chapter what culture is and how culture impacts your business.

Summary

As any business starts to grow it will experience problems; so-called growing pains. Most of the time people are the cause. I call it 'People Disease'. In my survey of business owners, I identified three main problems that were holding businesses back and preventing growth.

1. You struggle to recruit the right people

2. Employees don't do things the way you want them done

3. Employees don't have the same passion for the business as you

There is no pill that you can take to fix the disease, but there is an answer to these problems and it's called 'culture'.

Action steps

Take some time to think about the following issues:

- Does your business have People Disease? Which one causes you the biggest headache? What have you done about it?

- Find out how much People Disease is costing your business

- Which of the three problems can you identify with most?

CHAPTER TWO

What Is Culture?

Company culture is about values, purpose, beliefs, shared attitudes and behaviours: rules that are written and unwritten. In other words, 'It's how we do things around here.' It's what the company stands for. No business culture is the same. You can't look at another company's culture and copy it. It has to be about your business. Culture is made up of your company purpose, values, and the behaviours of your business. You could say it's the personality of the company. It's the DNA of your business; it's what makes you unique or, put simply, it's what makes you different from your competitors. Anyone can set up a business and copy what you do, but they can't copy your culture no matter how hard they try.

This is one of my favourite culture quotes:

'The only thing we have is one another. The only competitive advantage we have is the culture and values of the company. Anyone can open up a coffee store. We have no technology, we have no patent. All we have is the relationship around the values of the company and what we bring to the customer every day. And we all have to own it.'

HOWARD SCHULTZ, CEO, Starbucks

You may be thinking this culture stuff is all soft and fluffy, and I don't blame you for thinking that. But take a look at the companies who have a great culture and see their success, their happy employees and profits, and maybe you will rethink your opinion.

'This is not about fuzzy, holding hands around a campfire, kumbaya stuff. That's not what values and culture and mission is about. This is about building an organization for success. This is about winning. This is about doing the tactical things to make sure your organization and your people are aligned around the same thing.'

JUSTIN MOORE, CEO, Axcient

Perhaps you think that culture is something you don't want to introduce in your business. If that's the case,

I've got news for you. Every company already has a culture, but is it the culture that you want? Every business has a way of doing things that has developed over time. I'm talking about the way people are recruited, managed, communicated to or rewarded; how decisions are made and how employees are developed. For many companies nothing is defined. Everyone does their own thing. There is no structure, employees do their job the way they want to and go home. You may be annoyed at how employees do things or the way they treat customers. That is your culture.

The good news is that you can define the culture of your company.

- Is the current culture helping you reach your business goals?
- Will the current culture support your growth plans?
- Does your current culture have a purpose beyond making a profit?

As you employ more people you will see your culture start to drift. It's critical to maintain a strong culture for growth. Business owners who are really serious about their business growth realise the importance of having the right culture. Culture is as important, if not more important, than your business strategy. Why?

Because culture underpins everything you are trying to achieve in your business. Culture is the core of your business and it must be strong. Everyone knows what happens when you don't have strong foundations. Your business will become weak and start to crumble.

How culture impacts your business

The majority of business owners or leaders fail to understand how culture drives the performance of the business. Culture is reflected in many ways. These are just some of the ways culture impacts your business:

- How strong the shared values of the business are
- How far employees display the behaviours that support the values
- How employees treat each other
- How customers are treated
- How employees are recruited
- The way you communicate with each other
- The speed at which decisions are made
- Whether you become an employer of choice
- Whether the right customers are attracted to you
- How widely your brand becomes known
- How far everyone is working towards the same goal

Zappos is an online retailer, now acquired by Amazon, and is famous for its company culture. I asked Kelly Wolske, trainer at Zappos, how culture impacts the performance of the business. She said, 'It has a huge positive impact. We put culture first, and it is our belief and our experience that it is our culture that gives us the opportunity to create great experiences for our customers, our employees, our vendors and investors.'

A great culture creates employees who are engaged. Employees who are engaged make a positive impact on performance, which increases revenue and profit.

Some evidence on how culture and performance are connected comes from Queen's University Centre for Business Venturing.[1] Using data from employee engagement surveys and company results over a ten-year period it discovered the following for companies that had an engaged culture:

- 26% less employee turnover
- 10% more unsolicited employment applications
- 20% less absenteeism
- 15% greater employee productivity
- 30% greater customer satisfaction levels

---

1 *Best Small and Medium Employers in Canada,* 2014 study, Queen's University Centre for Business Venturing.

'I used to believe that culture was "soft" and had little bearing on our bottom line. What I believe today is that our culture has everything to do with our bottom line, now and into the future.'

VERN DOSCH, author of _Wired Differently_

A good culture creates a great place to work. As the business owner and leader it's up to you to create the culture of your organisation, but you can't do this on your own. You need your team around you to support you and to give their ideas on what it means to work for your business.

Now I'm not going to lie to you and tell you that creating a culture is easy, because it's not. It's hard. It takes commitment, dedication and focus. If you are serious about your business and are looking for growth then you need to devote time and energy to creating the culture of your organisation.

Many business owners put off developing their company culture. Why? Because it's an ongoing process. You don't just come up with a purpose and some values, tell everyone the values and expect it to happen and that's culture ticked off the list. That's the sort of business I worked in when I was an employee many years ago. There was a purpose and vision for the business, with values displayed on the wall. But no one lived those values so they didn't mean anything to anyone. The exercise had been completed, and they spent thousands of pounds designing posters to put everywhere, but it was a joke because the leaders didn't live the values.

Many business owners do exactly the same and then wonder why the culture fails. It's because they don't put in the time and effort needed and don't understand the importance of embedding a culture. If you want to be like the majority of business owners who struggle with staff turnover, have problems with performance with everyone pulling in different directions, then crack on. If you want your business to achieve success, if you're looking to scale or exit, then culture needs to be your priority.

If you want employees who will go that extra mile, who love coming to work, who tell everyone how great it is to work for your business, and where the best people are queuing up to work for you, then culture needs to be your priority. You see, culture is something you develop, measure and keep working at forever. If you want the success that you know you deserve, that your business deserves, then you must commit to doing this. Remember all the hard work you have done over the years, the late nights and early mornings, the weekends, the family events and parties you missed because you needed to get stuff done and no one else in your business 'got it'? It was all down to you. No one else understood why you were doing this.

Wouldn't it be great if the whole team understood and wanted it to work, wanted the business to be successful? It can happen and I can help you, but it's not for the faint-hearted. If you want to continue with your people problems and let the People Disease spread, then do nothing and it will spread. Trust me, I know. This is not a tick box exercise. It's hard work.

If you're thinking, 'Do I really need to create a great place to work and bother with this culture thing?', then you don't have the right mindset. You have two options: change your mindset and read on, or give this book to someone else.

How culture becomes a business asset

A great culture adds value to your business. When you are looking to sell your business, culture is considered an intangible asset. Company culture, either positive or negative, will soon become recognised by people outside of the business. When preparing your business for exit you need a positive culture. If you're looking to exit your business, the culture can't just be about you – otherwise it will fall to pieces when you leave. You need a strong culture, which will ensure that the business has a life beyond you. Company culture is an intangible asset of your business that you can't afford to ignore.

Unless you have been living in a hole in the ground for the last few years you will have noticed that the world of business and work is changing. For your business to survive, you will need to adapt. The future of the workplace is going to be different; the digital age is here and it's not going to go away. The workforce is changing. Baby boomers are now close to retirement age. The generation of people who wanted to have a job for life, a nice pension and additional holidays have nearly gone from the workforce. It's not like that anymore. The new generation, known as the 'Millennials', are here in the workplace. Born between 1980 and 1999, they are the largest age group to emerge since the baby boom generation. The accountancy firm Deloitte predicts this generation will make up 75% of the global workforce by 2025.[2] They want different things from the workplace and from their job. The days of people staying at the same company forever are not happening anymore. People want to have a career, develop and move on. They are not looking for a job for life.

---

2   Deloitte 2014 Millennial Survey.

Nathan Blecharczyk, co-founder of Airbnb, has over 2,000 employees. He says that in the technology arena in which Airbnb operates the competition for staff is intense.

In a bid to attract more millennials the firm makes it very clear what its core values are to help it stand out to would-be employees.[3]

> 'Millennials are known to be more purpose-driven, so as a company we're always communicating what our values are, both internally and externally, and trying to be true to those things.'
>
> **NATHAN BLECHARCZYK, co-founder of Airbnb**

Your mindset on how you treat and develop employees needs to change – I'll talk more about this in Chapter Seven. The new generation are constantly looking for ways to learn and develop. Too many owners won't spend time and money on training employees because they worry that they will leave and they see that as a waste of money. Instead, see it as a way to develop people while they are working at your business. You will gain from all the skills they learn so your business benefits. The new generation want more flexibility in their working hours and the location they work in. Allowing flexibility

---

3   *CEO Guru* series, BBC, Steve Tappin, 2016.

may seem difficult for you; you may feel like you are no longer in control. But flexibility can have a big impact on an employee's performance and their engagement level. They are not as interested in the material benefits. They want to feel valued and find purpose in the work they do. They want to understand how the work they do contributes to something bigger in the world. It's not just about the company making a profit.

If you want your business to still be here in five to ten years' time, you can't afford to ignore this. You will have to adapt your business to thrive.

At the time of writing this book there are huge changes on the horizon with the onset of Brexit. No one knows yet what Brexit will mean in terms of employing people from Europe. The latest figures from the Office for National Statistics show that net migration has fallen over the last year, as fewer EU citizens have come to the UK and the number leaving the UK has increased.[4] The number of EU citizens coming to the UK for work-related reasons has fallen over the last year, in particular those coming to the UK 'looking for work'. Does your business depend on workers from the EU? Are people still going to be coming from Europe to work in the UK, or is

---

4   *Migration Statistics Quarterly Report*, Office for National Statistics, February 2018.

that going to stop? If it is going to stop, you're not going to have such a big pool of people to pick from when you are recruiting. Employees will be able to be more selective and be able to choose where they want to go and work. Employees will be looking for companies that offer them the best choices, the ones that have clear values and purpose; companies that offer flexibility and development, where employees will feel supported and respected. In other words, the companies with a great workplace culture.

These employees aren't in it just for the money. I keep telling business owners it's not all about the money. To think that everyone is motivated by money is short-sighted. I'll discuss money and motivation in more detail in Chapter Six.

People are looking for something different. They are looking for purpose in their work; they have a desire to make a difference. They want to develop themselves and achieve their goals. They are looking for an employee experience. The sooner you can understand this and start taking action, the sooner you're going to move your business forward, start achieving your goals and create a culture where it's a great place to work.

Culture is critical to business success. Culture change takes time, it won't happen overnight. A great workplace culture makes you an employer of choice, where people will want to come and work for you. It strengthens your brand as an employer.

Now, you have two choices here. You can either be reactive or proactive – your choice. You can either let the culture evolve, as every business has a culture whether they want one or not, or you can design your own culture. You can decide what you want the culture to be, based on your purpose and your values. I don't want to oversimplify this as that makes it sound easy. It's not. There is a lot of work involved in creating a culture. But when you have a culture that everyone buys into, and values that employees understand and live, the transformation in your business will be amazing. Those problem employees we talked about at the beginning, with the symptoms of People Disease, can be cured by introducing the P.E.O.P.L.E.™ System. No step can be missed. Each one is important.

So where do you start? You start with the foundations. In Chapter Three I am going to introduce you to the People Foundations. I will explain the importance of the People Foundations and why this step must not be missed. Without the foundations in place you cannot recruit the right people. Getting the right people is key to building the right culture. Recruit the right people who will fit your culture and your business will thrive.

Recruit the wrong people and it will send your culture tumbling down. It then takes a long time to rebuild, which is why your People Foundations are key.

Summary

Culture is key to business growth. You cannot afford to get left behind. You need to start focusing on your company culture now. This takes years to embed, but you will see an impact before that, although it's not something that will happen overnight.

The workplace is going to look very different in the future. Employees want different things from work. Culture is not fluffy. Culture makes a massive impact on the performance of the business. Culture is an intangible asset.

If you plan to exit your business, you need a strong culture that will live beyond you.

Action steps

- Describe your current company culture in three or four sentences
- If you asked your employees to describe the company culture would they say the same as you?

- List ten things you would like employees and customers to say about your business
- Is your company ready for the workplace of the future or will you get left behind?

RECRUIT

Introducing 'Recruit'

How do I recruit the right people? I've lost count of how many times I have been asked that question by business owners. They really want to grow their business and understand they need to employ the right people to achieve that. Unfortunately they've had some bad experiences with the people they have recruited. This may be down to their lack of interviewing skills: they've just accepted 'yes' and 'no' answers, and not asked probing questions. Or they may have employed someone who is not right for the role, but they needed someone so they've made do with the best of a bad bunch because they couldn't face the thought of starting the recruitment process again.

You see, recruiting the right people is critical to your business growth. Without the right people on board you will constantly struggle, have issues with performance, poor teamwork, lack of engagement, high turnover and absence problems – it's what I call People Disease. The wrong people can create a toxic culture.

So how do you recruit the right people?

You need to recruit people who are aligned to your company values, who believe in your company purpose and who fit with your culture. If you don't, you will end up with high employee turnover, high training costs, customer dissatisfaction and disengaged employees.

> 'One of the most important considerations you must make is whether or not a candidate fits into your company's culture. The right person will build upon what you've created, but the wrong person can bring it all down very quickly – and culture can take an awfully long time to rebuild.'
>
> **RICHARD BRANSON**

The majority of businesses don't recruit against company values. Why? Because they don't know what their company values are, or their values are not clearly defined. They are not able to recruit people who fit their culture because they are unsure what their culture is. If they have identified their values, these have probably not been embedded into the business. In other words, the values are not lived.

In the next chapter I'm going to share with you the People Foundations you need in place, which include values. This will help you to identify your values so you can start to define your culture. Once your foundations are in place, you can start recruiting the right people for your business.

CHAPTER THREE

People Foundations

In this chapter I am going to discuss what I call the 'People Foundations' and explain why they are crucial to the success of your business. People Foundations are made up of your values, processes and systems, and they are key to making your culture a business asset. As the leader, the key is for you to align all of your people systems and processes around your values and purpose.

Some people think you need to find out your business purpose before you decide your values. I disagree. To me your values are fundamental to your business and don't usually change. They are what you believe in and what you stand for, whereas the purpose is about what the business is striving to achieve. Purpose is something you are continually aiming for – I will discuss this in more detail in the next chapter.

The People Foundations are often overlooked as they are not seen as the 'sexy' or exciting part of the business. You want to get on with the marketing, sales and strategy. The foundations are often left until last or, worst case scenario, the foundations are never laid.

Picture this: you and your partner have decided that it's time to build your dream home. It's been over five years in the planning. You have spent hours with the architect on the design and hundreds of pounds on the plans. You've finally found a builder and now it's full steam ahead. Wait. What if the builder said he could save you money and time, and get your dream house built quicker by not laying any foundations? Would you still go ahead? Would you spend hundreds of thousands of pounds on building a new house without foundations? No you wouldn't, not unless you wanted the house to come tumbling down.

So why do business owners put so much effort into building their business, spending huge amounts of money, having sleepless nights, suffering stress and missing out on life to build a business which has no foundations? All that hard work will be wasted when the business starts to crumble. Oh, it may be OK now, when there are only five or six staff, but as you grow the cracks will start to appear. What will happen to your plans to scale or exit?

Do you get the picture here? This is what happens in many businesses. The business is set up and there is so much to do – the sales, marketing, finances and employing staff. You are so busy you ignore the basic foundations. Putting your People Foundations in place gives you a solid base on which to build and scale your business. Let's take a look at what needs to be included in your People Foundations. The first part is your core values.

What is a core value?

To recruit, inspire and retain the right people in your business you need clearly defined company values. Values define the rules and boundaries of the business. They make up the company culture and its personality. Your core values remain fixed. If something in the business is not working, then it's the business strategy that changes. If things are going well in the business, or things are going badly, the core values remain constant. You don't compromise on your values.

> 'Determine what behaviours and beliefs you value as a company, and have everyone live true to them. These behaviours and beliefs should be so essential to your core that you don't even think of it as culture.'
>
> **BRITTANY FORSYTH, Vice-President of Human Relations, Shopify**

Some companies express their core values as a noun. Personally, I prefer a phrase or short sentence as this gives more clarity to the value. There is no limit on how many values you have, but take into consideration that you want employees to remember them so having ten or twelve can become difficult.

To give you an idea of what I mean by core value phrases, here are some examples:

First, our values at my company, J Mann Associates:

- Do the right thing
- Take ownership
- Work as a team
- Continuously improve
- Create a great workplace

Infusionsoft values:

- We genuinely care
- We build trust
- We own it
- We learn always
- We check ego
- We dream big
- We win together

Zappos values:

- Deliver 'Wow!' through service
- Embrace and drive change
- Create fun and a little weirdness
- Be adventurous, creative and open minded
- Pursue growth and learning
- Build open and honest relationships with communication
- Build a positive team and family spirit
- Do more with less
- Be passionate and determined
- Be humble

Having your values as a phrase gives more meaning that just using a noun.

Business vs personal values

It's important to understand and clarify your personal values. Your personal values are what you believe in. There are no right or wrong values and everyone's values are different. Problems arise when you are in conflict with other people's or company values. When I worked in a company that paid lip service to values, I was unhappy. I realised it was because my personal values conflicted with the company values. My personal values and the company values were not aligned. If you have staff who are unhappy, conflicting values could be one of the causes.

When I coach leaders, part of the coaching process I go through with them is identifying their personal values. This can seem quite an alien experience to many people who have not thought about this before. It's important that you know what your own values are.

They don't need to be the same as the company, but they do need to be aligned. If they conflict you are going struggle.

The first step is to identify your personal values. This will take some time and you do need to give it some thought. You can find a worksheet on values for you to complete at www.jacquimann.com/resources. Here are some questions for you to answer to help you clarify your personal values:

- How much importance do you place on the role of values in your life?

- What five values are important to you?

- Of these five values, which three are the most important to you?

- Which of these is the single most important value for you?

- How does your life reflect your three most important values? Give examples.

- Do you ever think, or feel, that you might not be 'living up' to your values?

- Do you experience any conflict of values?

Once you have established your values it's time to look at the company values.

How to define your company values

If you are serious about building a great business, the first step is to define your core values. You can start by answering the following two questions:

1. What is important at your company?

2. What is unique about working at your company?

Defining the core values of your business is not an easy task. It's not something that can be done in ten minutes but it needs to be done. You can't leave it to chance. No one said it was easy, which is probably why most business owners don't bother; it's too difficult. Unless you are just starting out in business, this is not something you should do on your own. The best way to define your company values is to involve your staff.

A huge thing to remember is that culture is not something you do to people, it's something you do with them.

I've seen many business owners spend days writing the company purpose and values. They present it to the team and wonder why no one is excited or buys into the 'culture'. To make this work you need to include them in the process. This can be done in many ways. If the business is fairly small you could include all staff. If that's not possible, you could put together a culture team. You could run group sessions to get people's ideas. If you put the effort in your business can be transformed. Once your core values are defined you need to commit to them. Everything you do in the business then needs to be aligned to your values. Values can transform your business into a great place to work, create your company culture and that culture can then become a business asset. When I talk about being aligned I mean making sure everything you do reinforces your values and your purpose.

Why values are key to culture and success

Values set a foundation for the company culture. They help to improve the morale and can make employees feel proud of the company. Values help to align employees around specific behaviours, and influence how they interact with each other in the workplace. Values give people direction and provide a road map of where the business is going. When you clearly understand your values, everything you do within your business revolves around them – customer service, new products, new equipment, decision making and hiring and firing. If you're surprised by that, don't be. You see, this is how you get everyone working together as everyone understands what is expected when they work at your company. Remember problem number three – employees don't have the same passion for the business as you? This is how you start to solve that problem.

Many business owners don't like confrontation and find it difficult to discipline or confront employees about their unacceptable behaviour. Values makes this much simpler for you. Instead of saying 'that person isn't doing the right thing' and it making you feel uncomfortable, you can ask how that behaviour demonstrates the company values.

Dan Ralphs, dream manager at Infusionsoft, said, 'Whenever there is a violation of our values – and they are deep enough at Infusionsoft – it's really obvious and it makes everyone feel uncomfortable. If somebody is doing something that is blatantly selfish, everyone in the company says, 'What? That doesn't feel like us, that seems off'. It becomes really obvious to everyone, which is how you want it to be. That's the way you take the time to preserve your culture.'

Define your behaviours

Once you know your values, you need to define three or four behaviours that demonstrate those values, for two reasons.

1. Behaviours become measurable, which makes managing people much easier
2. The values and behaviours become your culture – it's what differentiates your company from all the others

Behaviours make it easy to define the standards that you want to see in the company. Behaviours make the values tangible, which you can then observe and measure. If values are not measurable it is difficult then to hold employees accountable.

Here are some examples of the behaviours at J Mann Associates:

VALUE	BEHAVIOURS
Do the right thing	Go with your gut instinct
	Say no if it's not right for us or the client
	Always be honest with each other and clients
Continuously improve	Go out of your comfort zone
	Think differently
	Find solutions
	Challenge and stretch yourself
	Find a better way

For each company value, brainstorm the behaviours that you want people to demonstrate. Select three or four per value. Now test each behaviour to see if they are measurable and observable. If not, cross them off and move to another one until you find the right behaviours.

Recruiting against your values

Does recruiting against your values help? You bet it does. The question I am often asked is, 'How can I recruit the right people? There are no good people out there.' There are good people out there; you are just not attracting the right ones. Don't think it's just about the salary either. Owners say they can't afford to employ the good people. It may come as a surprise to you, but not everyone is motivated by money – more on this in Chapter Six. To recruit, inspire and retain the right people in your business you need clearly defined company values. Only recruit against your values, even if the candidate has a glowing CV. If they don't match your values and you recruit them, you are setting yourself up for disaster.

> 'We believe that it's really important to come up with core values that you can commit to. And by commit, we mean that you're willing to hire and fire based on them. If you're willing to do that, then you're well on your way to building a company culture that is in line with the brand you want to build.'
>
> **TONY HSIEH, CEO, Zappos**

Once you know your values you can use these in your recruitment process. This will go a long way in keeping out problem staff. I know I am repeating this, but your recruitment process needs to be aligned to your values.

Over the years I've seen disasters with recruitment. The thing I can never understand is how little time and planning some business owners put into recruiting.

In most businesses employees are the single biggest contributor to the business. Owners need employees to get their business to where they want it to be. If that's the case, why do they give recruitment so little time?

To recruit the right person there are several things you need to do. The first is to recruit against your values. Include the values in your job advert – make sure people know about your values. When you receive CVs, make sure you read them before you invite that person for interview. Don't leave it until five minutes before they arrive or you call them.

I recommend an initial telephone interview asking questions based on your core values and if that goes well invite them in for interview. By carrying out the initial screening you save yourself – and the candidate – a lot of time if they were never going to be the right fit. If they don't pass that interview, if they are not the right fit with your culture, you don't take their application any further. You will know by their responses if they are the right fit for you or not.

On the day of the interview make sure your questions are prepared. Ask more questions based on your values, then move on to the technical questions. You might ask the technical questions or get a member of your team to carry out this interview, or you may do the interview together. Where possible I always recommend involving someone else in the interview process to gain another view point.

Once the formal interviews are out of the way, it's time for the candidate to meet the team. This can be done in several ways. Team members can be invited into the room to have a chat with the candidate. Or candidates can visit each department, the managers show them around, explain what they do and ask if they have any questions. Another way is to have a lunch and invite all team members to meet all candidates at the same time.

The objective of this is to get feedback from the rest of the team on the candidate. You will be surprised at what some people say or do when they are meeting the teams. They think the interview is over. Meeting the team is essential if you are recruiting for a manager who will be leading a team. People's behaviour can be strange sometimes, and not at all what you would expect.

Strange behaviour

Several years ago, I designed and ran a full-day assessment centre for a client. They were recruiting for a head of HR. There were eight candidates on the day, each of them taking part in various exercise and interviews. I had asked the HR team to join us for lunch. This gave the team the opportunity to meet their potential new manager and for the candidates to meet their potential team. I was slightly surprised when one of the candidates, who was doing extremely well on the exercises, went over to the lunch, selected some sandwiches and went and stood in a corner and spoke to no one. That is not the sort of behaviour I expected. Just in case you are wondering, she didn't get the job.

Over the years I have interviewed hundreds of people. I've trained on numerous interview techniques, but no matter how much training someone has had you can't, and should never, ignore your gut instinct. If a candidate answers all the questions correctly and has glowing qualifications but something doesn't feel right, go with your gut. Don't make an offer if your gut is telling you something is wrong.

The start of the People Disease cure is getting the right people on board who believe in your values and can demonstrate the behaviours you are looking for.

Your values need to be on your website for people to see. Make it clear what it's like to work in your company. Some companies add videos to their website with employees talking about what it's like to work there.

I asked Dan Ralphs, Infusionsoft's dream manager, about their recruitment process and how they recruit against their values. He said, 'Honestly, the first thing we're screening for is whether or not they fit the values. Secondarily we'll take a look at the resume. This will tell you generally whether or not they have the qualifications necessary; if they have the tools that we need. What the resume won't tell you is whether or not their values fit. We do our very best to screen for that right away, and then throughout the process. If you're not a values fit, you won't get hired. In every interview after that, whether there's a four interview process or a five interview process, the question at the end, when everyone syncs on their experience with that person, is are they a values fit? If they are, then awesome. We can look at the other criteria. But if they're not, that's a hard no.'

I've included some examples of interview questions based on values. They will, of course, depend on what your company values are, but this will give you an idea of what I mean. The recruitment process is an opportunity to show how values can be used so you have confidence that you will select and invest in the right people.

Value: Work as a team

- Tell me about a time when you achieved a successful result through the actions of a team?

- Give me an example of a time when you experienced conflict within a team?

- Have you been on a dysfunctional team? What did you do as a team member or team leader to address the problems?

- What's the biggest challenge you face being part of a team?

Value: Continuously improve

- Tell me something you have learnt over the last six months

- What is the last book you read? Would you recommend it to me? Why/why not?
- What were some areas of development in your last feedback session? What did you think of that and what did you do to improve?

Value: Do the right thing

- Tell me about a time that you did what you thought was right to get the job done, even though it may have been against popular opinion?

Value: Exceed customer expectations

- How are you gathering feedback from your customers and how do you use this feedback?
- Tell me about a time where you wowed a customer

Value: Take ownership

- Describe a time when you weren't pleased with your work and why?
- What personal or professional mistakes have you learned the most from?
- Tell me the last time you missed a deadline? What were the consequences?

During the interview, look for their willingness to learn and their ability to fit in with the team. Do they ask insightful questions about the job and the company? Do they show that they are open to learning? Have they researched the company? Do they understand the company purpose?

While you can teach people new tasks, you'll have a hard time changing their personality. To make sure you are recruiting the right people, and to make this work, you need to be completely committed to the values. Only recruit against your values. If the candidate doesn't match your values and you recruit them, you are setting yourself up for problems.

Core values formalise a company's culture. The most important thing is that once you know your core values you commit to them, and everything you do in the business should be aligned to your values, including your procedures, systems and rules. I know I am repeating myself here, but I can't stress enough how important this is.

Recruiting from within

Recruiting internally is something that is often over-looked and can be a big mistake. If employees see people from outside being recruited into positions they have not been made aware of they will become disengaged. Recently I was talking about the difficul-ties of recruiting with a nursery owner. I asked her if she advertised roles internally and she looked at me shocked. The thought had never occurred to her. This nursery has a high turnover of staff and this could be one of the reasons. Staff often leave the business for a promotion or a different role. Why wouldn't you promote from within? Promoting people internally has the advantage that they already understand the culture and values, have relationships with the team and it promotes a positive work environment.

Can you see how important it is to have a recruitment process? If you don't have a process, anyone who recruits in your company will be doing it differently. You need systems and processes for doing this. If you exit the business and there are no processes, people will be recruited who don't meet the values and the culture will start to crumble.

Processes, systems and rules

Many companies skirt over these essential processes, and suffer as a result. You see, things such as your employment contracts, employee handbook, sickness and absence procedures, rules for taking holiday, grievance procedures etc. create the rules of the workplace. If you're a creative, entrepreneurial business owner, it won't surprise me if you find these foundations a little restrictive – even frustrating.

In any business, HR processes and procedures must be up to date, fit for purpose and set up to give you, the business owner, the flexibility to do what's best for the company. The clue here is in fitness for purpose. Processes and rules create unified standards that ensure all employees are treated fairly. More importantly, everyone understands what they need to do to ensure consistency.

Many business owners wrongly believe their employees know what to do and what's expected of them. A lack of processes, systems or procedures leads to inconsistency – in behaviour, performance, discipline, and results. When staff are seen to 'get away with it', resentment builds, which slowly kills morale and encourages poor performance. Remember the second problem in my survey in Chapter One – employees don't do things the way I want them done? Maybe you have an understanding of why now. I've worked with so many owners who complain about this problem. When I go in to the business to help cure their People Disease, I discover nothing is written down; it's all in the owner's head. I tell the owner that employees are not telepathic. How do you expect them to know what to do, they can't read your mind.

If you mention HR to most owners they think of policies, procedures, employment law and lots of red tape. Ok, I admit there is some of that, but there is so much more to HR than people realise. HR is about developing people and working with the business from a strategic perspective to support growth. Business owners will need more HR expertise to support workplace culture in the future. Many business owners believe that by having policies in place, it will stop them doing the things in their business that they want to do. That's not true. Policies and procedures need to be designed around the company, and the 'rules' should be in line with the company culture and values.

I meet many business owners who don't have employment contracts in place for their staff and they have been in business for over ten years. This is madness. Why? Because you are not protecting your business. Your employment contract will contain clauses that will give your business protection. Not only that, it makes it very clear from the beginning to both parties what the expectations are. The amount of times I have had to resolve issues for owners when the relationship has gone wrong; it can become costly. So much of it could be prevented if the foundations are right at the beginning. I don't want to get into too much legal detail, so let's look at it this way. When everything is going well at the beginning of the employment relationship it's great, but when the relationship turns sour that's when you wish you'd paid more attention to the really boring stuff, like the employment contract.

I hear many business owners say they don't like having rules, people can make their own decisions. Everyone knows what's expected of them round here. It's that telepathy thing again. I have news for you: they don't know what's expected. It may surprise you, but the majority of people like to have rules. They like to know what they can and can't do. It's also good for your culture, because new employees understand very quickly 'how things are done around here'. This is also where your behaviours fit in.

Rules don't have to be a novel. I know one business where their rules all fit on an A4 sheet of paper. It's what suits your business and culture. Without rules you are not able to manage performance as no one knows what's expected. A huge downside is that good employees will soon become demotivated if they perceive other employees are not following the rules. The knock-on effect of this is that the good employees often leave.

The basics – contract, handbooks, procedures and rules become the basis for your culture. This includes what clothes you wear to work, the hours of work – are they 9–5 or flexible? Can employees use personal mobile phones at work to make calls and interact on social media? These are things that you need to decide and these will start to define the culture of your business.

A workplace with rules has defined boundaries, expectations and consequences. Underpinned by the core values, the HR processes and systems help support the business and make it a great place to work. That's why you need to get these foundations in place before you can begin to implement the P.E.O.P.L.E.™ System.

Once you've found the right employee, it's time to bring them on board.

The importance of a great induction

Why is induction important? In the induction you need to talk about the culture and values and how they underpin everything you do. From the very first day you must start to embed those values with employees. What happens in the business, what their role includes, what the culture is about, what the values are, what the expectations are, what the job involves, and how it's going to work. In theory, that sounds great, but in practice it doesn't always happen the way that it's meant to, because most companies don't spend the time putting together a good induction process for new starters.

I was speaking at an event recently to a room full of business owners. I started talking about induction and said, 'This is a typical company induction. On their first day, the new starter is shown around the building and introduced to the team. You explain where the toilets are, where the kitchen is, if there is one, and the coffee machine. Then you show them their desk, go through health and safety, fire exits, go through some procedures, the employment contract, and make sure they're happy with that. You explain lunch breaks, dress code or uniform, and then most people will expect the starter to get on and do the job. Sound familiar?' I looked around the room and everyone agreed that this was how they carried out their induction. I'm sorry, but that's lazy and does not give the new employee a great introduction to the company. How can they understand your company culture from that type of induction?

In organisations where there is a great culture, a culture where people want to stay, where people want to work, a lot of time is spent on the induction process. When I say a lot of time, I mean between one and four weeks in some cases. Often, people have to start from the beginning no matter what their job. They don't come in to the business and do their job from the start. They actually have to learn what it's like to work at the business from, say, answering the phones. You need to think about all the different things that you can add into your induction process. It goes without saying that you need to include values in your induction process.

It depends on the size of the organisation as to how much time you can let that person not be doing the role that you have employed them to do. But it is short-sighted not to think about the upside of inducting a person into the business properly and explaining the purpose and values in detail. Remember what I've said. These are your foundations. These are the things you need to get right from the beginning, right from the start. Explain to people how things are done here. Get them to buy into what your values are and how behaviours are measured. Tell them how it works and what you expect from them. Get other employees involved in the induction, explaining about values and how it's a great company. This also gives employees the opportunity to leave at any time during the induction stage if they feel it's not right for them.

Trust me, this is much better than going six or seven months, or even longer, and then realising this person isn't a fit for the company and you're going to have to say goodbye to them. By going through a really good induction process, employees will see whether this culture is something they want to be part of.

At Infusionsoft, they have a week where they focus on purpose, values, mission and fitting into the culture. They teach employees about their unique vocabulary and things like the Infusionsoft 'high five'. They teach them what it means to be an Infusionite, which is a special name for their employees.

Dan Ralphs says, 'They also take part in a culture quest. They wander around the building asking employees questions: Where is the dead end staircase? Who has been here for more than five years? We talk about our leadership model and each one of our values in depth. They have to memorise the purpose and values. We spend a lot of time on culture.'

During the induction process, Zappos and Infusionsoft offer money to employees to leave at the end of the induction period if the employee doesn't feel that this is the right company for them. (I'm not suggesting that you have to do that.) If they refuse the money, Infusionsoft ask people for a written response to explain why they are refusing the money.

The induction is one of the keys to your People Foundations. Make sure you have a robust induction process in place. Think about all the things that need to be included, but, importantly, base it around your culture, your values, and 'how we do things here'.

At J Mann Associates, we have a four-week induction process. Week One is about the company, our values, processes and systems. Employees are given a four-week timetable, which outlines what will happen each day, who will be carrying out the training and any actions that the employee needs to take. For example:

On Monday at 2pm the employee reads the client's probation procedure. On Tuesday at 10.30am, Janine (people advisor) will provide training on the client's probation procedure. It's important that the employee reads the procedure before they have the training as this give them an idea of what is involved. The new employee shadows Janine to make sure they have a full understanding of the process, with the opportunity to makes notes and ask questions. The employee is given tasks and once Janine is confident that the process is followed, the new employee can then carry out the work.

I hope this explains why you need to get these foundations in place before you can begin to implement the P.E.O.P.L.E.™ System itself. These are the building blocks that are critical to your business success.

Summary

The People Foundations are critical. All your people processes and systems need to be aligned to your purpose and values. Knowing what your personal values are is important. You need to ensure that your personal values are not in conflict with your company values.

Work with your team to clarify the values for the company. Once this is done, align all of your processes and systems to the values. People like rules, processes and systems.

Not having the right People Foundations in place will cause the company to crumble as you grow.

Recruit against your values. If the qualifications look good but they are not a good values fit, don't employ them. You will live to regret it. They could turn your culture toxic. Recruit internally where possible.

Induction is really important. Many companies don't spend enough time on induction.

Action steps

- Complete the personal values exercise
- Get your team together to start the process of identifying your company values
- Review all your people systems. We call this a 'people check-up'
- Review your employment contract, HR policies and processes – are they aligned to your values?
- Review your recruitment procedure – is it values based?
- Are your values on your website? Do you ask values-based questions before or during the interview? Are you advertising vacancies internally?
- Review your induction procedure – what changes do you need to make?
- What can you implement that will help a new employee understand the culture of the company?

CHAPTER FOUR

Purpose

What is purpose?

Now the foundations have been laid, it's time for the first step of the P.E.O.P.L.E.™ System – purpose. There are various names for purpose. Some people call it 'vision' or 'your why'. I prefer 'purpose'. Purpose answers the question of why. It's the reason you get out of bed in the morning. It's the difference you are making in the world; it's why you do what you do every day. A company purpose should be something you are always striving for but may never achieve.

As the business owner, it's your job to provide the direction for your company, you are the leader. It sounds obvious, but few owners take the time to get clear on the real reasons they are in business. If you're serious about attracting the right people, you need to define and communicate your values and your purpose. Not everyone is in work for the money. Your purpose – along with your core values and behaviours – will translate into your culture. Culture impacts everything, from the people you attract, to the work that gets done, to the results you are able to achieve.

A company purpose has very limited use if only you, the business owner, or your top team understand it. Purpose can have a transformational impact when it is explained in the right way. You need to communicate your purpose to all employees.

Our company purpose at J Mann Associates is 'to make every business a great place to work, where employees are inspired, engaged and find purpose in their work'.

Research by Deloitte has found that businesses with a strong sense of purpose are more confident about their growth prospects.[5]

Focusing on purpose, rather than profits, builds confidence and investment. So what do I mean by a strong sense of purpose? Employees want to understand the purpose of the company. They want to know:

---

5   *Core Beliefs and Culture Survey 2014*, Deloitte.

- What does the company stand for?

- How does their job contribute to the company purpose?

- How does the company purpose impact customers and society?

Knowing your company purpose will also attract customers who believe in what you believe. Your purpose is what makes you different to your competitors, and this is what creates a competitive advantage.

Problems occur when your purpose is not aligned to your values. Once you know your purpose you need to commit to it, be consistent and ensure all areas of the business are aligned to the purpose.

As I mentioned in Chapter Two, the millennial generation want to know the purpose of your company. They want to know what your business is giving back to the world, the environment or the causes your business supports. Your purpose is your reason for being.

Let me ask you this question. Are all your employees clear on why the company exists, and can they clearly explain it to customers? If I came into your business now and asked your employees what the company purpose is, would they be able to tell me? Would they all tell me the same thing? If employees don't know why the company exists it's probably because of one of three reasons.

1. You don't have a purpose statement at all

2. You don't have a clear, inspiring purpose statement

3. Your internal communication of the purpose is poor

Your purpose statement needs to be clear, inspiring and compelling, and describe what your business does every day.

Remember you can't just stick a few words on a bit of paper and put it on the wall. That won't work. A purpose statement needs to be:

- Clear about what your company does

- Clear about who it does it for

- Clear on employees' end goals

- Clear on why customers should care

So, either start your purpose statement or review your current purpose statement and see if it delivers all the points above.

How to define your company purpose

1. Look at three or four of your company values. What do you, as a company, really care about?

2. What do you want your business to be known for?

3. How do you make a difference to your customers' lives?

4. How are you different from your competitors?

5. What are the goals of the company? Which ones matter most and why?

6. Why does your business exist, beyond financial gain?

Answering these questions will provide the information you need to define your company purpose.

Now you have established your company purpose and values, you need to find out where the business is currently with the culture. Where are you now and where do you want to get to? Once you have done this exercise you can identify the gaps and create a plan.

Where are you now?

The exercise I carry out with my clients is to get the business owner and senior team, if there is one, together and ask them questions about what currently happens in the business. It's the 'where are you now?' stage.

This can be a difficult exercise. For it to be effective you need to be brutally honest about how it really is in your business, otherwise you are wasting your time and nothing will change. I tend to ask the following questions:

- What's it like to work here?

- What systems and processes are in place?

- How effective are the systems and processes?

- How easy or difficult is it to recruit?

- How do people speak to each other?

- Do people work as a team?

- What is the environment like to work in?

- What hours do people work?

- How long does it take to make decisions?

- How engaged are your staff?

Do you get the idea? You really need to drill down to discover what the behaviours and the culture are really like now. Not what you want them to be like, but what they are currently like.

Take your time

I was working with a client on this exercise. They were getting very impatient with me spending time on the 'where are you now?' stage. They were more interested in getting to the 'where do you want to be?' stage. After 15 minutes, the leader said, 'That's enough, let's move on'. I explained that there was no point in moving on with the exercise if we couldn't cover all the areas of 'where are you now'. The reason he wanted to move on was because it was painful. He was feeling uncomfortable. He really didn't want to acknowledge what was actually happening in his business. He was embarrassed. They wanted my help to define and create their culture, which was why I was there. I wasn't about to give up so we carried on with the exercise. This exercise can show up serious areas in the business that you have been ignoring or avoiding doing anything about.

You need to do this in detail so when you do the second part of the exercise you will be able to identify the gaps. If you don't know what's wrong or what's not working at the start, you can't fix or change things. As this process identifies all the work that needs to be done to get your business and culture where you want it to be, it can be overwhelming for some people. I never said this was going to be easy.

Where do you want to be?

Imagine it's five years from now. How do you feel when you walk into your company? I will ask similar questions at this stage, but the team can tell me what they want it to be like. This stage is much easier for most people.

Before you look at the gap between 'where you are now' and 'where you want to be', there is another stage, called 'what is really going on?'

What is really going on?

This might seem a strange question to ask, but many business owners don't have a clue about what is really going on in their business. They think they know what's going on. They think they understand how their staff are feeling, how motivated they are, what they are happy or unhappy about. They think they know what makes people tick, what career aspirations people have. But do they really? Honestly, hand on heart, do you know? Can you imagine what a difference it would make to your employees and your business if you knew the answers to all these questions?

There is a very simple way to find out how your employees are feeling and that is to ask them. There are various ways to do this – there are hundreds of online employee surveys you can get them to complete but I'm not a lover of these. If you are going to use an online approach don't use it in isolation. Back it up with face-to-face meetings. I'm much more in favour of the good old-fashioned way – talking to them.

My reasoning behind this is when I go into a company I give the employees a short questionnaire. One of the questions is 'Are the company values alive?' They can give an answer on a scale of one to five, five being the highest. Most employees give an answer of four or five. If you're using this approach to measure culture this would be a good score. You would be happy with that. When I interview the employees, I say to them, 'The questionnaire asked, "Are the company values alive?" and you gave it a score of four. Can you tell me what the company values are?' The majority of the time they don't know what the values are. There are two possible reasons for this: 1) there are no values, or 2) if there are, they are not clearly defined.

So I hope that you can see from this why I'm not in favour of just using online surveys. They won't necessarily give you a true picture of what is really going on.

This is an exercise I have carried out many times for clients. After talking to the business owner, I then write a list of questions that I am going to ask the staff. These are not questions set by the business owner; I set the questions based on my conversation with the business owner and from what I discover at the 'where are we now?' stage.

For the next step, I ask the client to send me a list of all employees. I select who I would like to meet, let them know what day I will be visiting or calling, and ask them to select a timeslot. This is an exercise you can do yourself, but if you want to get real, honest feedback you would be better getting someone completely impartial, preferably from outside the business, to carry out the meetings with staff.

I make sure the employees understand that whatever they say to me is confidential. Any feedback given is anonymous, unless the employee specifically asks me to mention their name. It's important that it's anonymous because often employees won't open up and discuss things with me if they think it's going to be reported back.

It's important to put the employee at ease. Depending on the current culture of the organisation they might think I am going to go straight back and tell the boss everything. You need to build a rapport with people so they trust you. I always ask everyone the same questions.

A skilled interviewer will be able to probe when asking questions – probing enables you to gather more information. Now don't get me wrong, some people will moan and groan about the company, but, again, a skilled interviewer will be able to spot these issues and find out who the whingers are and what the real issues are. There will be a pattern. Spotting the pattern is the key to discovering the underlying issues that staff have in the business. Most of the time, as the business owner, you will be blind to these issues.

When I feed back to the business owner no names are mentioned. This exercise is not for the faint-hearted; you might not like what you hear, but you must take action on the feedback. If you don't take action it will speak volumes about you as a leader. It's essential that you put a plan in place to address the issues raised in the feedback. You need to speak to staff and explain what is going to happen since you've received their feedback. If you do nothing with the feedback, there are three outcomes.

- Staff will become cynical and think it was a waste of time

- You will be just like other business owners who say they want to do things but don't; your business won't move on and you certainly won't create a great place to work

- Your culture will never become a business asset, but it may become toxic

When I said you need to be able to take the feedback I wasn't joking. I mentioned earlier that business owners think they know what's really going on. This stage is often where you get the wakeup call and find out that your perception is wrong. I recently spent a day in the business of a successful entrepreneur. I chose the questions I wanted to ask employees based on my conversation with her. At the beginning of our conversation she said, 'I think things are OK, now. Much better than they were.' Needless to say, things weren't better, they were worse. To give her credit she took the feedback well. She was, however, surprised to discover that some of her staff were frightened of her and didn't find her approachable at all. The fact she started to take action straight away was great. The thing she missed though was that she came up with ideas with only one other member of staff. To make changes you need to involve staff and get their ideas and input, which will give more buy-in.

When you are looking to change culture and introduce new ideas, to be successful you must include as many staff as possible. Do it *with* them and not *to* them. You will be surprised by how many good ideas they have and how different those ideas are from yours. You see, you can only assume you know what they want, what they value and what they believe in. But that's all it is: an assumption. The only way to find out is to ask them and include them.

Don't fall into the trap of assuming that you know how to fix the issues. Your idea may not be theirs.

You may be wondering what sort of questions I ask the employees. It is different for each business, but to give you an idea here is a selection that you can use.

- How do you feel about the company at the moment?
- What is your understanding of what is going on in the business currently?
- Do you have any concerns?

- What do you think or feel would help?

- On a scale of one to five, one being the lowest, how motivated are you to come to work?

- How motivated do you think other staff are on a scale of one to five?

- What are your thoughts on the amount and type of communication you are receiving?

- Do you have a clear progression path?

- Do you have regular meetings with your manager?

- What should the business start doing, stop doing, and continue with?

- What do you tell your friends and family about working here?

- What are your views on the current leadership team?

- On a scale of one to five how much, if any, has the leadership team improved in the last six months?

- Anything else you would like to add?

What is the gap?

The next step is to gather all the information from 'where are you now?', 'where do you want to be?' and 'what's really going on?' This will identify the gaps.

If I am working with a client I will meet with the team again, discuss the findings and help them put together a plan on how they are going to fill the gaps. This isn't something you can or should do alone. You need your team members to help you.

I've now covered the foundations and the purpose, which you need in place before you can start on any other step of the P.E.O.P.L.E.™ System. In the next chapter I will discuss the environment and how that plays a big part in company culture.

Summary

Purpose is what makes you get out of bed every day. It's the reason you are in business. Employees want to understand what the company purpose is and how they contribute to that. Purpose is something you are striving for but many never achieve. Everything you do in your business is driven by your purpose.

Looking at your business and identifying where you currently are against where you want to be in the future will give you the gaps. Feedback from employees will provide more information on what is really going on from their perspective. As the owner you may have an idea of what is happening in your business, but it may not match the reality of what is going on.

When you make changes, always include employees in the process. Don't assume you know what they want.

Make sure you always act on any feedback.

Action steps

What is your company purpose? Do you have one? If you do, is it clear? Does it inspire employees? Does it need to rewritten? Have you communicated it to everyone?

Carry out these three exercises:

- Where are you now?
- Where do you want to be?
- What's really going on?

Work with your team to discuss the gaps. Create your plan to move forward.

CHAPTER FIVE

Environment

In this chapter I will discuss what I mean by environment, the second step of the P.E.O.P.L.E.™ System, and the impact the working environment can make on an employee's performance and the business. I have a couple of questions for you:

• How does it feel to work in your business?

• Is it a great place to work?

You see, we often take our working environment for granted. Most of us will spend the majority of our life at work. Let's look at environment surroundings first. When you see things every day you don't always notice your surroundings or people's behaviours.

When you go and visit somewhere for the first time, that could be a business, a hotel, someone's home, what do you notice? Which of your senses kick in? What do you see? What do you hear? What can you smell? What do you feel? Is the place tidy, scruffy, dirty or immaculate? Are there boxes piled high, files lying around, clutter everywhere, or does it look organised? Does it look like they have just been burgled?

Whenever I go anywhere I always notice smells. It could be a good smell. One of my clients has several hotels and there is always a beautiful smell as you walk in to the hotel. But not all smells are good. Some are strange, even unpleasant. It makes me wonder if the toilets are blocked or if a cat has died in there. When I leave the place I come away thinking, 'What was that smell?', not 'What lovely people, let's do business with them.' Whenever I think of them I remember the strange smell. I'm sure that's not the impression they wanted to make.

First impressions

A few weeks ago I carried out a 'people diagnostic' (this is where I go into a business and interview the employees) for a business owner. The owner really wanted to look at the culture of his business. After travelling over an hour to get to the client's office I needed to use the toilet. It was 10am. What greeted me when I entered the toilet? The paper towels in the bin were overflowing, I could write my name on the windowsill in the weeks' worth of dust and the toilet hadn't been cleaned for weeks. This was a staff toilet. It was not a good environment and not a good first impression for me. What message is that giving out to staff? Is that saying we value our staff? I don't think so. This all forms part of your culture.

I hope you are starting to get the picture here. When people, whether its clients, customers or employees, visit your premises for the first time they will notice things that you take for granted. You see these things every day and it becomes the norm. You forget that what people see when they walk through the door gives them the first impression of your business and often the last impression. To create a great place to work you need an environment where employees are happy, feel safe and can have fun.

The workplace environment affects the mood and performance of your employees. It also influences who fits in and who doesn't. That's why you need to think about the type of culture you want. Are you serious, fun, creative, or a flamboyant company? Is your company dress code aligned to your culture? Dress code can have a big impact on employee attitude. The workplace environment is your opportunity to express your unique identity, so make sure it reflects what your company stands for. Don't copy another company's culture. What does your working environment say about you as a company or business? Have you looked around you lately?

Workplace surroundings

Here is your challenge. Walk into your business as if it was the first time. Walk in with fresh eyes and see what other people see, hear, smell and feel. What do you notice? What is the decoration like? Is it faded, is paint peeling off the walls or is it dirty? Are the colours consistent with your brand, or hotchpotch? Are the posters up to date? Do they look professional or are tatty copies falling off the wall? Is the furniture old and worn, or is it bright and new? Is it too hot or cold? Are the kitchen facilities clean? Is there rotting food in the fridge? What about the systems and the technology in your business? Are you behind the times? Are you moving to the digital age or still in the Stone Age? Are employees sharing equipment? What does it feel like? Is there a strange atmosphere? Are employees happy, stressed or do they look miserable? Is there a smell?

Think about your company values for a moment. Does your working environment live up to those values? If it doesn't, now is the time to take action.

A few years ago I was working with a company on their culture change. After going through the 'where are you now?' and 'where do you want to be?' exercises we identified a huge gap. There was a definite 'them and us' culture between senior staff and the other employees. The chief executive made a commitment to the staff to create a culture where they all felt like one team. Can you imagine my surprise when several weeks later I drove into the car park and saw car park spaces allocated to the senior management team with their names on little plaques? That type of behaviour does not create an environment aligned to the culture that they said they wanted. Is your environment aligned or out of sync?

Remember, times are changing. Employees are going to be more selective about where they want to work. They will have lots more choice about where they want to work. Employees want to feel valued and if the environment is in conflict with your values you are going to struggle to recruit. Poor environments can affect the performance of staff. It can increase levels of absence, hinder innovation and affect retention rates.

Google is well known for its work environment. It has been described as an adult playground and not a place of work. This environment works for Google but that doesn't mean your business has to copy this. Your culture is unique, you are not Google. Providing a great work environment doesn't mean you have to buy bean bags, provide free breakfast, lunch and dinner, or have video games and football tables around the place. These are perks of working for a company. If people want to come and work for you just because of the perks you offer they are not the right people. You want to employ people who want to work for you because they believe in your purpose and values. The perks are a bonus.

Unifying teams

Recently, I was giving a talk to business owners on workplace culture. Later, I was chatting to some of them over lunch. Sunny Sandwell from Sunshine Events told me that they have an amazing office culture, which they have created over many years and people always comment on it. As the business developed, they became aware of a different culture in their logistics and events teams and that they felt separate from the other teams. This was against their overall vision and they realised they had to act to bring it back on track. As they worked on a separate site and away at events, they needed a different approach to help. Over time, they met with the team to understand how they felt and what was missing before launching the solutions. They branded the buildings throughout the business to match and be of the same style, swapped team members so they could appreciate what the others did, improved communication with weekly memos, drop-in sessions and online groups, together with organising more out-of-work

> activities. This helped blend the culture and solve the initial problems identified to continue with their culture in a business where Sunny said 'people are our greatest asset'.

This is a great example of how to include employees in the process. You must always remember, if you have more than one site you need to be consistent. It's not just for the customers to see; it's for your employees to work in.

Employee behaviour

How people speak to each other in the workplace is hugely important. Are they speaking to each other in a friendly way or do you cringe when you overhear them? Do they even speak to each other? Many years ago I worked with a company who had 'communication problems'. There was one department where all employees were on edge waiting for the director to arrive each morning. How their day would be depended on whether he greeted them when he arrived or ignored them. The worst part was he walked past his entire team to get to his office. Some days he would ignore everyone. If this happened he would appear miserable all day and hardly communicate with anyone. If and when he did communicate, it came across as rude or dismissive. You could argue that the team were responsible for how they reacted to him; they were in control of how they felt. However, it was a regular occurrence and it was wearing the team down and creating an unhappy work environment.

This didn't say much about the amount of trust in the team, as they didn't feel they could approach him about this. I'll talk further about trust and why it's important in Chapter Eight.

I was asked to coach the director on his leadership style and communication. I asked him if he was aware of how he affected his team when he didn't acknowledge them, not even to say good morning. Interestingly enough, he didn't realise he even did this. His team thought he was rude. His response was that he was deep in thought and trying to resolve a problem. Through his coaching, we were able to address this and help him raise his self-awareness.

Are you starting to see how employee behaviour affects the working environment? Environment is not just about bean bags and free food. This type of behaviour does not create a great place to work.

Do you have people in your business that others avoid or put up with? Do people say, 'That's Pete, he's always like that'. If you do, what are you going to do about that person? Are they displaying the behaviours that align with your values? People who don't align with your values can make a culture toxic. You need to make a decision about the individuals, which can mean saying goodbye. If you continue to ignore it I can guarantee you will regret it later.

Silos

It can be easy for 'silos' to appear when you have teams, especially if they are based on different sites or different floors in a building. Teams within the same company can develop their own culture. I was asked to merge two teams into one. I went into a company that had two finance departments – each department worked on a different customer contract. The company had lost a big contract, which meant that the two finance teams were going to be merged. Some people would unfortunately lose their jobs and be made redundant. What I needed to do was look at the culture of the teams. It was interesting that these two departments, working for the same business, had completely different cultures. Can you imagine what it was going to be like when they had to merge?

Different styles

One leader was indecisive and liked to have lots of chitchat with her team. She always wanted everybody to be happy about any decisions that were made, and, in fact, didn't really make any decisions – her team made the decisions and she went along with them. As long as everybody was happy, she was happy – not a great leadership style. In contrast, the other manager, who was a bit of a bully, would boom out questions and answers to everyone and tell everybody exactly what they were going to do. She would also keep lots of information to herself so that the rest of the team didn't know what was going on. She tried to control everyone by keeping them in the dark. Her team found her intimidating and some were frightened of her.

Two very different leadership styles and two very different cultures within the same business – how can that happen? This company had identified their values and purpose, but that's all they had done. They were not living the values, as managers had set up their own cultures within their teams.

Another interesting thing was the company used a lot of acronyms. I did an exercise with both teams on the meaning of the acronyms. Amazingly, they meant different things to each team. Often when you go to work in a company they have acronyms that they use and when you've worked in a different organisation they mean something else, I understand that. But these people worked for the same company. Work was also needed on their processes. Their processes were different and they even recruited in a different way. I spent several weeks with the teams mapping out the processes. How can departments or teams in the same business be so different?

I'd like you to look around your business and start to notice what is going on. Are there silos in your business? Do sales and marketing do something different to finance? Do the admin team do something different to the marketing team? Look at all the different areas in your business and see if they have their own individual cultures. If they do, what are you going to do about it? Can you see the impact this could have on your culture? To have a successful culture, everyone needs to be aligned to the values and behaviours.

When I worked in manufacturing, the company had three buildings on one site. It didn't take me long to realise that they worked in silos. I needed to do something about this. The customer service team was always complaining about the packing department in a different building, saying that they didn't get orders out on time. This was an opportunity to get them to spend time in each other's departments. Employees spent a day in the other department to see how it worked. This helped them to understand the difficulties they each faced. They were able to work together to resolve the issues and it created better working relationships. It worked so well that I introduced it for every department and it became part of their development plans.

I see this happen often, when employees only understand their own job and department. This doesn't help engagement or enable everyone to support the company purpose.

Arranging for employees to spend time in another department or in other areas of the business will help them learn more about the business and how it works as a whole, not just what goes on in their own department. This also encourages employees to get to know each other better and build relationships.

Trust

What is trust? Employees want to work in an environment where they feel safe and where there is trust. One way to start to build trust is to create an environment where employees feel they can speak up without worry or fear of criticism or judgement. Allow them to speak up about any issue or concern or idea they may have. Encourage them to notice when things in the business are not aligned to the purpose and values. Have an open door policy where employees are encouraged to discuss things that are on their mind. This is a great way to build trust and open communication.

In Chapter Eight I will discuss the leader's role in creating the culture and how trust plays a big part. When there is trust, employees feel safe. This is a feeling, it's not something that you can see or touch; employees feel it in the environment.

'Trust: Firm belief in the reliability, truth, or ability of someone or something.'

OXFORD ENGLISH DICTIONARY

Trust is not something that will happen overnight. As the leader you must be:

- consistent in what you do

- build relationships with people

- listen to what people have to say

- deliver results

- have clarity on what you want to achieve

Paul J. Zak, Harvard researcher, has spent decades researching the neurological connection between trust, leadership and company performance.[6] He compared people at low-trust companies with people at high-trust companies. Here are his findings for companies with high trust:

- 74% less stress

- 106% more energy at work

- 50% higher productivity

- 13% fewer sick days

- 76% more engagement

- 29% more satisfaction with their lives

- 40% less burnout

---

6   Zak, P (2017) *The Trust Factor: The Science of Creating High Performing Companies*, New York, Amacom.

Another way to build trust is to encourage employees to take risks and to learn from their mistakes. Some companies have awards for failure. Accounting software company Intuit gives a special award for the Best Failure and holds 'failure parties'.[7] Co-founder Scott Cook explains that 'every failure teaches something important that can be the seed for the next great idea.'

Sarah Blakey, the founder of Spanx and now a billionaire, credits her father for her success.[8] She said her father would ask her at dinner each night, 'What did you fail at this week?' This redefined failure for Sarah. 'Instead of failure being the outcome, failure became not trying. And it forced me, at a young age, to want to push myself so much further out of my comfort zone.'

Employees want to feel safe and secure. You can read more about safety in Chapter Six, when I discuss Maslow's Hierarchy of Needs.

7   Stewart, Henry, '8 Companies That Celebrate Mistakes', Happy.co.uk. blog (8 June 2015).

8   Friedman, R (2015) *The Best Place to Work: The Art and Science of Creating an Extraordinary Workplace*, New York, Perigee Books.

Have fun

It's important to have fun at work. At Zappos, they like to create an environment where people can thrive. They have a team that plans events but Kelly Wolske, trainer at Zappos, said, 'We find that events that just pop up are more popular. For instance, the second floor challenged the third floor to office Olympics and we did a bunch of silly games. Way more fun for a lot of people than maybe a carnival organised in the courtyard.'

The majority of people spend most of their time at work, so you need to enjoy it. There are different ways to create fun at work. It's important to remember, though, that not all ways will be right for your culture. Do what is right for your company.

Find different ways to introduce fun into the business. Ask your employees what ideas they have. Remember, you need to include employees in the decisions as this will help build engagement.

2.30pm disco

I know one company that everyday has a 2.30pm disco. I spoke to Pete Cann, owner at Back-2-Front Chef, to find out more about the disco. Pete said, 'The 2.30pm disco was born when I felt flat in the office one afternoon. I turned up the radio, got up and started to dance. This then led me to encourage the team to stand up and have a dance with me. Not everyone bought into the idea initially. However, once we had a chat about the benefits of moving during the afternoon slump we were all soon looking for a tune to dance to. Getting everyone on board was a real eye opener and it meant it was not just me driving the dance.

'Next I bought a disco light that plugs into a timer switch on the wall. Every day at 2.30pm it goes off and we all get up and dance. It's been in place for over a year now. We've changed the song twice – each time was when we had a new starter, so we got them involved in the decision process too. Has everyone been up for it? No. Funnily enough, those people are not with us anymore. The disco is always performed during the on-job experience time, after an initial interview, and always mentioned during the interview to gauge the future employee's reaction.

'Would I recommend getting everyone up and moving after lunch? Hell yeah! The proof is in the numbers.'

Are you creating an environment where people can perform at their best? Your environment is part of your culture and your brand, but it is often overlooked. Do employees want their friends to work at the company? How great would it be if employees say to people 'come and work with us'?

Now you are ready to move on to Step Three of the P.E.O.P.L.E.™ System: ownership.

Summary

In this chapter we looked at the importance of the workplace environment. It's not just about having free food or bean bags; there is more to it than that. Remember, free food is a perk.

Environment is about the atmosphere, the decoration, the cleanliness, the smell, the feel of the place. More importantly, does your environment match your values?

Your environment needs to be aligned to your brand.

How employees greet and treat each other affects the working environment.

Different departments may have become silos, creating their own cultures within them. The working environment needs to feel safe and there needs to be fun and trust.

Action steps

Carry out the exercise on walking into your business as if it were the first time. Pay attention to what you see, hear, feel and smell. Note it down. Review your findings and identify the areas that are not aligned to your values.

Ask team members to carry out the same exercise and see what they notice.

- What are your next steps to make the changes that are needed?

- Do you have any silos? What are you going to do about them?

- What things could you do on the spur of the moment that would be fun?

INSPIRE

Introducing 'Inspire'

To retain the right people in your business you, as the leader, must be able to inspire your employees. Inspired employees are far more productive.

Stay true and focused on your purpose. You need to be engaged and passionate about your company purpose. Motivate and energise people towards your purpose.

> 'Inspire: To make someone feel that they want to do something and can do it.'
> **CAMBRIDGE ENGLISH DICTIONARY**

Set clear goals, celebrate the wins, have fun and learn and laugh together. Give employees the enthusiasm to achieve their goals.

Appreciate your people, learn to give praise and say a simple 'thank you'.

You must deliver and walk the talk. Do as you say, be approachable, trustworthy, listen and be honest. Be authentic: employees will know if you are pretending to be someone you are not.

CHAPTER SIX

Ownership

What is ownership?

First of all, I'm not suggesting that you make employees part-owners in your business. I'm talking about giving them a sense of ownership. When employees feel a sense of ownership they treat the company as if it were their own. Ownership, Step Three in the P.E.O.P.L.E.™ System, is about taking the initiative, making decisions and being accountable for those decisions. It's about standing up and saying, 'I will do that'. To be able to take ownership, employees need to be motivated and feel safe. Core values are at the centre of successful companies where employees take ownership.

Ownership is about taking responsibility, being accountable and doing the right thing, which is guided by your core values. When employees take ownership, they take accountability for that task. They understand that what they do, or don't do, can affect others. If they don't deliver on their part this could prevent the team or the business achieving a target or goal.

> 'A true "ownership culture" is one where employees feel a substantial, personal stake in the company's performance. It creates a situation in which behaviour is guided more by values than by rules, even when "nobody is watching".'

OLIVER WYMAN, Management Consultants

To take ownership an employee needs to be motivated. So what motivates people? If you think it's about money, you are wrong.

It's not all about the money

This may surprise you, but not everyone is motivated by money. Employees like to be rewarded for doing a good job but they are not always looking for money as the reward. Many business owners ask me about reward schemes and bonus structures and they spend hours putting complicated plans together and then tell me they don't work. Do you know why? It's because the rewards and incentives that are introduced are what the business owner thinks the staff want to receive, not what the staff actually want.

Without question, money can be a massive motivator. In turn, a financial bonus or a pay rise can be a powerful way to recognise and reward brilliant performance, but only if that employee is motivated by money. Otherwise it won't work.

One of the downsides to giving money as a reward is that the employee does not get an experience. Let me explain what I mean. The employee achieves their targets or goals and gets paid a bonus. The money goes straight into their bank account along with the rest of their salary. They spend it, like they would their salary. What's the difference? There is no experience for them to remember. If, instead, you arranged for the employee and their partner to go to a five star restaurant or bought them a pair of VIP tickets to see their favourite pop star, what experience do you think they would remember more? The meal, concert, or the money going into their bank?

So what does motivate people? Let's take a brief look at one theory of motivation.

Motivation

For employees to take ownership of their work, they need to be motivated. There are several theories around motivation, Abraham Maslow's theory probably being the most well known.[9] Many years ago, I remember studying Maslow's theory of hierarchical needs for my Chartered Institute of Personnel Development (CIPD) exams. Maslow wrote his psychology theory in 1943, and it's still popular and relevant today. In case you're not familiar with his theory I will give you a quick overview. Maslow's theory is that people are *wanting* beings: they always want more and what they want will depend on what they already have.

Maslow suggests that human beings' needs are arranged in a series of levels in a hierarchy of importance. This theory is often depicted as a pyramid. There are five levels to the pyramid. Starting at the bottom of the pyramid you have basic needs:

1. Physiological needs – food, water, warmth, rest, oxygen, sleep

2. Safety needs – security, safety, freedom from pain or physical attack

---

9   Mullins, L J (2010) *Management and Organisational Behaviour*, New Jersey, Financial Times Prentice Hall.

The next level up on the pyramid is psychological needs:

3. Love – sense of belonging, friendships and intimate relationships

4. Esteem – accomplishment, achievement, reputation, respect

Self-fulfilment is the fifth level:

5. Achieving your personal potential – self-actualisation, personal growth

Maslow's theory is that once the lower-level needs are met, giving more of the same does not provide motivation. People will go up the hierarchy as each lower level is satisfied. Once a human's basic needs are met – food, safety and security – people will progress to the next stages. Safety, as you can see, is one of the basic needs. A leader's role is to create a safe environment. There are lots of arguments for and against this theory. Some people may get their needs met through work, some in other areas of their life.

The old motivation methods of the 'carrot and stick' are no longer effective for many roles. A carrot and stick approach means you offer people a reward to persuade them to do something, and punish them if they refuse or don't achieve the task. This is known as extrinsic motivation.

Intrinsic motivation is far stronger for many employees these days. Intrinsic motivation is about being driven to do something because you believe in it or because you feel it's the right thing to do – not because you receive a reward, but because it is personally rewarding. Can you see how intrinsic motivation fits with employees wanting to work for a company that has a purpose? It's not just about the money.

Ownership needs initiative

> 'Initiative: The ability to use your judgement to make decisions and do things without needing to be told what to do.'
>
> **CAMBRIDGE ENGLISH DICTIONARY**

Initiative is not something you can train people in. I say to managers when they are interviewing that if someone shows initiative, recruit them. You can train them in how to do the job but you can't train someone to have initiative.

You need employees who show initiative as these are the people that will take ownership. When an employee takes ownership of a task, they are taking on the responsibility to complete the task and to get the required result for the business.

If an employee volunteers to take ownership of a task, that is fantastic. Don't then make the mistake of micro-managing them. This will cause them to feel demotivated.

Decision making

Once you have clarified your values, and your purpose is in place, people will really understand what the business is trying to achieve and will start to take ownership for moving things forward. They need to know how far they can go when making decisions.

The values should be defined well enough so that employees know the right things to do when they need to make a decision. In day-to-day operations, if an employee is not sure whether they need to ask their manager for permission to do something, they should be able to look at the company values and know if it's the right thing.

Giving ownership means allowing employees to make the decisions on how they do that job – remember, don't micro-manage them. I was talking to an owner recently who was having problems with his manager. When the owner was away from the office he received endless telephone calls and messages from the manager asking him questions on what he should do next. The owner found this frustrating and said he'd told the manager when he was out of the office the manager must make the decisions. I challenged him about why the manager could only make decisions when he was out of the office. Why not all of the time? The owner realised that he needed to step back and let the manager make decisions, even if he was there, otherwise the manager would never take ownership.

You need guidelines and parameters on what is acceptable and how far an employee can go. Again, this needs to be defined by your core values. Let's look at an example. If you have a customer complaint, what can an employee do or how far can they go to make that customer happy without having to refer it to their manager? What do your values say about customers and how you treat them? Give employees authority. No employee wants to be running backwards and forwards to their boss every five minutes to check that it's OK to do something. It's frustrating from an employee perspective and even more frustrating for a customer. If, like me, you've had to wait in a shop or been kept on hold while they just 'check' with their manager about an issue before they can do something, you will understand how frustrating it is. For many employees, if they don't feel they have any authority to carry out their job, they will leave the company. These employees are often the people you want to retain. Enabling employees to take ownership has the added benefit of freeing up your time, meaning you no longer have to deal with every little issue.

Giving employees responsibilities can help them to feel valued. When employees feel valued they become more engaged in the business. Why do you need them to be engaged? More on that in Chapter Nine.

Trusting employees and giving them authority to make decisions will have a huge impact on your business. It allows employees to solve problems and come up with new ideas that can then be shared with the rest of the team. Allowing employees to take ownership gives them greater satisfaction and stops the customer from feeling frustrated by being passed from pillar to post. I think we have all experienced that and it's not great when you are on the receiving end. Can you see how creating ownership can produce better customer service? What impact would this have on your bottom line?

Are you worried employees might get it wrong or do something that you don't approve of? When employees can make decisions they can be innovative and find new ways of working, which can be shared with everyone. This again can have a great impact on the business. You have to learn to let go and trust them. If you keep checking up on them every five minutes this won't work. This is where your company values are key. Remember your values are how you do things at your company. Any decisions that are made need to fit with the company values.

Communication is important in a company where you want employees to take ownership. Employees need to understand how they fit into the bigger picture and how, by taking ownership, they are contributing to the company purpose and helping achieve their goals and the company goals.

Reward and recognition

When employees do a good job it is important that you reward them. Zappos have a co-worker recognition scheme. Each employee can give out a $50 bonus to anyone who may have done something out of the ordinary or wowed someone. Kelly Wolske said, 'Being able to give that recognition to peers gives people a sense of purpose and connection to their work.'

It's not the only option; remember, it's not all about the money. In fact, you could find that more creative rewards have a far greater impact on the individual in question and overall team morale. The key here is to discover what drives your staff and then reward appropriately. Taking the time to find out in the first place sets you apart from most managers because it shows you genuinely care. For example, some individuals may want recognition. Others may want position or authority. Others may want new opportunities or the chance to develop further. Remember, just ask what they would like, don't assume it is money.

Recognition for a job well done is what some employees want more than money or gifts. Give employees credit for a job they have done well. Recognising an employee in front of the rest of the company can have a huge impact on their engagement level. This could be done at a team or company meeting. Sometimes, employees just want you to say thank you. By doing this you are acknowledging that they have made a difference and they will feel valued.

Several of my clients have Employee of the Month awards. There are several ways that you can do this. One is to ask employees to vote for another employee. This could be because they have delivered great customer service, for living a value, or going above and beyond. Or it could be based around targets or achieving a goal. These do have to be managed well because they can become a bit stale and employees lose interest.

You could introduce little cards that employees can send to each other saying 'Congratulations'. I worked in a company where you could send employees a card which said 'You're a star'. It did make you feel great when you received one in the post from one of your colleagues.

Giving employees ownership will have a massive impact on your business. When employees believe in and understand the purpose of what they are doing, they want to take responsibility to get things done.

Employees also want to develop and that's where Step Four of the P.E.O.P.L.E.™ System comes in: progression.

Summary

Money is not a motivator for everyone. In fact, the majority of people are not motivated by money.

Let people take ownership of tasks. When employees take ownership they use their initiative and they become accountable for the task. They understand that if they don't deliver on their task it can prevent the team from achieving a goal.

Don't micro-manage or you will demotivate people. Set clear guidelines based on your values about how far employees can go to resolve an issue or come up with a new idea.

Reward and recognise employees for good work and for demonstrating behaviours based on the company values.

Action steps

- What three things can you do to increase employee ownership in your business?

- Find out what motivates your employees

- What do you currently do to reward or recognise employees?

CHAPTER SEVEN

Progression

What does progression mean?

In this chapter I am going to cover Step Four of the P.E.O.P.L.E.™ System and explain what I mean by progression, and the importance of progression for employees.

Progression links to motivation, purpose and ownership. Employees want to progress, but if there is no sense of purpose as to why they are doing it, they are not going to be motivated. Can you see how all of these steps are linked together? Putting one step of the P.E.O.P.L.E.™ System in place is not enough. You need to have them all.

What progression paths do you have in place in your business? When people think of progression paths they imagine it's for employees who want to become managers. Now, your business may not be big enough to have lots of managers. That doesn't mean you can't progress people within the company in different roles, give them different projects to work on or train them in new skills. Not everybody wants to be a manager anyway. If employees do the same job day after day, there is a huge risk that they will become disengaged.

Do they know they can progress?

I was talking to an owner who said they have lots of opportunities within their business for employees to progress. They can start as an assistant, move into a team leader role, progress in qualifications, take on a specialist role and undertake further development to become a manager. Brilliant, I said. How do you communicate that to employees? She looked at me blankly and then had a light bulb moment – she didn't tell them at all. She waited to see if an employee asked if they could do some training. What they could actually do is include this as part of the recruitment information they send to candidates and then discuss this at the

---

interview. They could have posters around the building or in staff rooms showing the different routes for development and how employees could progress in their career. None of this is hard, but it does go back to the telepathy again. Employees are not mind readers; you must communicate with them all the time, over and over.

Kelly Wolske from Zappos said, 'We really encourage the teams to actually write their own progression plans so that it's meaningful to them and makes sense. A small team is not necessarily going to grow at the same rate as the company and not everyone can become a manager. It's more about broadening skills or taking on bigger projects. Each department works to build their own so it's not one-size-fits-all. There are paths for folks who want to become people managers versus developers who want more complex projects.'

If management is not an option, think about what else you could be offering employees. What other opportunities can you provide for them? Perhaps employees could spend time with a more senior employee and work on a specific project to gain experience? Maybe there is a certain task they enjoy and you could give them the responsibility for that specific area?

'Train people well enough so they can leave, treat them well enough so they don't want to.'
RICHARD BRANSON

The millennial generation are looking for training and development within a company. This is where your mindset needs to change. Most employees are going to leave the company at some stage. Owners say to me, 'Why should I train them up and pay all that money for training when they're going to leave?' My answer is yes, they probably will leave, especially those in the millennial generation. A job isn't for life anymore. They don't want jobs for life. They want to gain more experience and move on after a few years. I'm not saying that they will all leave; you will retain some of them. You need to look at this differently. What benefits can the business get from developing these people while they're here? If you don't train them, they're going to leave anyway, so train them and benefit from that training; they get experience and are given the opportunities. Provide the training and development opportunities so that they don't want to leave your business. Training people makes them feel valued. It means you are prepared to invest in them, not just with money but also with your time.

Staff will leave your business to progress and develop if they are not given that opportunity to do that in your company. What's even worse is if you train people and then don't give them the opportunity to apply for other roles in your business to use their skills. Then they will mostly likely leave.

Cast your mind back to the company I talked about in Chapter Two – remember, the company that didn't live the values? They paid considerable amounts of money to train me but never gave me the opportunity to use these skills. I was told to carry on with my job, I didn't have the experience to be promoted. Instead, they hired people from outside the company. It wasn't just me that this happened to. How do you think it made me feel? Frustrated, undervalued, demotivated. Guess what happened?

You're right, I left. I got a new job with a company that valued me, one where I could grow and use my skills. Skills that my old company had paid for. They were the ones that lost out. I was prepared to stay with them but they stifled my development. Don't make that mistake. I remember the day I left the company the HR director gave me flowers. He said, 'Jacqui, what advice would you give me when taking on new staff?' I replied, 'Don't spend your money on training new people if you're not going to let them do the job, but thanks for paying for mine'. He didn't know what to say to that.

Progression is about finding ways to develop employees. You might have ideas on what you would like them to do, but what are *their* aspirations? The easiest way to find this out is to ask. It's as simple as that.

My favourite way of finding out how employees want to progress is in a one-to-one meeting. I recommend monthly one-to-one meetings with your employees where possible. If you have a large team then monthly may not be possible. Employees like to have regular one-to-one communication and feedback. Having these regular meetings allows you to get a better understanding of your employee, what their plans are, where they see themselves in twelve months' time, and set realistic objectives. It's also an opportunity to review the core values and behaviours – more on that later. Let's look first at annual appraisals and why I don't recommend them.

The dreaded appraisal

I am not a big lover of annual appraisals. They are dying out in companies, especially in companies where they are working to create a great culture and to increase employee engagement. The majority of annual appraisals are a complete waste of time. I attended a conference earlier this year on the future of work. The audience was asked if they still held annual appraisals. Out of an audience of nearly 200 people only three put up their hands. Many people in the audience said they had stopped them as there was no value in them. Managers found them a chore.

When I worked in the corporate world it was always something managers and employees hated. The dreaded appraisal. I remember when you got the invitation to say 'It's appraisal time, it's time for our twelve-month review', and everybody's heart sank. They knew what was going to happen. Their manager would go over all the things that had happened over the last twelve months, start criticising their work, tell them all the things they've done wrong and then set some objectives for the next twelve months.

I never saw people come out of these appraisal meetings feeling motivated and inspired. Managers saw it as a tick box exercise. They would complete the appraisal form, set the objectives, ask the employee what training they needed, then file it. The next time the appraisal form came out and got dusted off was for the next appraisal meeting twelve months later.

If you still feel you really need to do an annual appraisal, remember the 80/20 rule: make sure it's 20% looking back, 80% looking forward, but for goodness sake, review it every three or six months. You see, to me, the annual appraisal does not support people's progression. By the time you review it everything has already happened and you can't change it. It's a bit like an end-of-year meeting with your accountant; it's all over, you can't change it.

One-to-one meetings

One-to-one meetings provide regular two-way feedback. This is the time to take the opportunity to discuss an employee's progress. These help with employee progression as they are up to date and in line with the business objectives and goals. Things change so quickly in business these days, you can't afford to wait twelve months. In a one-to-one meeting, you and the employee can work on what is relevant right now.

Seven steps to a great one-to-one

So what does the ideal one-to-one meeting consist of? I recommend to my clients the following – nothing too complicated or onerous, otherwise it won't happen.

1. Start by reviewing the objectives from last month. Some may have been completed, some may be ongoing. If they have not been completed discuss why.

2. Ask what things are going well. Get the employee to answer first, remember it's a two-way process. Getting the employee to respond first gives you the opportunity to hear how they feel things are going. Depending on their response you may need to adapt or change the way you were going to approach the session.

3. Ask what's not going well. This could be something in their role that's not going well that you could help them with. Give them more support, provide training or get a team member to help them. It could also be an issue with the business or something that is causing a hold up or a blockage that you are not aware of. This can then be reviewed by you or the employee and a solution found.

4. This is one of my favourite questions, as you can get so much valuable information from this: what

should the business start, stop or continue doing? Also ask this question on a personal level. What should the employee start, stop or continue doing?

5. Values and behaviours. Ask the employee to score themselves against each value. This will help the employee to understand which core values are their strengths and which they need to improve on. Ask the employee how they think they demonstrate the behaviours or where they feel they need to improve.

6. This is a great opportunity to give an employee recognition for positive behaviour. Give them specific examples of where you have seen them live the values. Discuss the behaviours they need to focus on and again give specific examples. Ask the employee for ideas on how they could improve their behaviours.

7. Progression. Where do they see their future? What do they want to be involved in? Where do they see themselves in twelve months' time? This is also a useful tool to give you an insight into whether an employee intends to leave in twelve months to travel the world, for example. This gives you the opportunity to prepare and start succession planning. There may be another employee who you can start progressing, ready for this role. This saves time and money on recruitment by replacing

someone internally but has the added advantage that they already understand your culture.

8. Set objectives for the next month, with outcomes and deadlines.

I recommend about an hour for a one-to-one meeting. Stay focused. Don't get distracted.

Summary

Progression is important to employees. They want to understand how they can learn and develop.

Change your mindset. Employees are going to leave the company at some stage but how can the business benefit from their skills while they are employed? Train employees, then find ways that the employee and the business can benefit from the training.

Unless you really have to carry out an annual appraisal, ditch it. One-to-one meetings give a much better insight into how an employee is progressing, what their aspirations are, and they can help with succession planning.

Understand the benefits of regular meetings with employees and review how they are living the values.

Action steps

- Set up regular one-to-one meetings with your employees

- Brainstorm ways you can progress employees

- Decide how you are going to make employees aware of the progression path available

- How are you going to support the development of employees once they have received training? How can the employee and business benefit?

CHAPTER EIGHT

Leadership

It all starts with you

I'm assuming as you bought this book you have the passion and you want your business to succeed, which is great. As the leader you are the driver. Let's move on to the fifth step of the P.E.O.P.L.E.™ System – leadership.

You are the person who will create, drive and develop the company culture. This is not something you can delegate to a senior manager or another member of staff. You have to lead. There's no way you can delegate the responsibility. You can share it, but you need to drive it.

There has been so much written about leadership that it's hard to decide what to include in this chapter. There are many attributes that are needed to become a good leader. My focus is on the skills you need as a leader to engage employees and create that great culture. To ensure your culture becomes a business asset you need to create a culture that is going to live on after you have left the business. This is especially important if you are planning to exit your business. Building the culture takes time and commitment. Only people who have a real passion to make this happen will succeed. Once the company values and behaviours have been defined, you have to live them. You have to walk the talk. That can be hard for some people. You can't expect employees to live the values if you don't.

> 'Be the change you wish to see in the world.'
> **GANDHI**

If you want to create a great place to work and a company where people are queuing up to come and work for you, you have to be a great leader and role model. I am sure, like me, you have experienced leaders who are excellent with words. They can motivate you and inspire you. Then you spot them a few weeks later doing the opposite of what they said. The problem is, their actions don't match their words. You know that old saying, 'Don't do as I do, do as I say'.

I never said this was going to be easy. It's not just in the workplace either that you need to live the values and walk the talk: it's in your private life too. You never know who is watching you or who you might meet when you are out and about. Your behaviours need to be congruent with your values. To be honest, if you are the sort of person who behaves differently outside of the workplace then there is little point in trying to create a great workplace culture that is different from you. You must be true to your own values. This is why it's important that your personal values are aligned to the company values, which I talked about in Chapter Three. If they are not, it will never work. You will be in conflict with your values. Culture is hard work and a continuous effort. If you think you just need to come up with a purpose and values and pop them all on a poster, forget it,

As the leader, you must walk the talk. If you are not seen to be buying into and living the culture then your employees won't either. The focus here is on 'seen'. I know I've said this before but I'm going to say it again, adding words to a poster on a wall and talking about values at company meetings is not enough.

- How are you demonstrating the company values?
- What do employees see you do that demonstrates you are living the values?

- Are your behaviours congruent with the values?

- How often are you communicating the values?

- When you make a decision, it needs to be based on the values

Every piece of communication that you send out needs to have some reference back to the values. Everything in the business needs to be based on the values. I hope you are getting the message here. As a business owner this can make decision making easier. It's easy to be distracted by the next new shiny thing or idea. It might look exciting; you could give it a try. But wait, stop. Does it match the company values? Is it aligned to the company purpose? If you answered no to the questions then you have your answer. Decision made, don't get distracted by things that are not aligned to your company purpose. Walking away from short-term gains that are not aligned to your purpose shows you have a strong commitment to your purpose. Making values-based decisions sends a strong message about the importance of your values, purpose and the integrity of your leadership.

Sometimes as a leader you can make assumptions that people understand what's happening. Because you understand what's going on you think that everyone else understands too. You need to ensure that all your communication is clear on what you are trying to achieve and that employees understand where they fit into that. If they really don't understand what's going on, you're not going to get the engagement. Employees might have questions they want to ask you, so be open to answering those questions.

You need to give praise and recognition to employees when they do a good job and this needs to be linked to a value. The same can be said when an employee is underperforming. Link this back to a value too. Some people find this easier as they don't like confrontation. Linking the poor performance or behaviour to a company value removes the personal aspect.

Get a coach

As the business owner and leader, if you don't have a coach you're seriously undermining your potential. Now I know that this is a bold statement to make, but it's something I've personally experienced and passionately believe. I'm certain my business would look entirely different if I hadn't invested in regular coaching over the years. Plus, I know the difference that even just a handful of coaching sessions makes to my clients. I'm not saying that you can't be successful without a coach. That definitely isn't the case and I'm sure you've met people at the top of their game who've achieved amazing things with little help. But these people are the exception. The fact is, most successful people have a coach. Just take one look at the sporting world and you can see this is true.

Coaching is beneficial at any stage of your business journey. For example, if you're just starting out, you'll find the right coach will become a trusted sounding board to help you get direction, focus and clarity. In comparison, if you've been in business a few years, a coach can help you reassess your direction and clarify your future path.

It needs to be the right coach. What's more, the right coach will hold you to account. If you say that you'll do something and you don't, the right coach won't let you get away with sorry excuses and explanations. That's because these excuses keep you small and stuck. Implementation and action kick-starts your progress and takes you to the place you need to be – and that's what your coach will motivate you to do.

A coach will challenge you and encourage you to answer the really hard questions. A good coach will be able to see beneath the surface because they'll read your body language and the subconscious cues that you're trying to hide.

The benefits of coaching

First of all, you should expect a return on investment. Just like your other business investments, coaching should deliver tangible deliverables. These are likely to be related to how you feel – but more importantly, what you're able to deliver in your business.

You should also expect to develop a better understanding of yourself, as you increase your self-awareness. You'll find that your comfort zone will expand as you successfully try things and you'll have a feeling of being more successful and more capable. You may also find that your goals get bigger as you come to realise just how much you are really capable of achieving.

Feedback on your behaviour is key as a leader and often no one in your business will give you really honest feedback, but a good coach will.

Understanding your leadership style

It's important you understand your leadership style and how it impacts on your effectiveness. There are several ways to do this. With my clients I recommend a leadership assessment where you discover your leadership strengths, challenges and areas for improvement, all measured against best practice. For those of you who want to find out what your teams think of your leadership style I recommend a 360° assessment.

What is a 360° assessment?

As a leader it can be difficult getting feedback on your behaviours. Employees might be frightened to speak up in case they lose their jobs. They might feel intimidated or don't know how to approach you. Not many employees will tell the boss that their behaviours are not living the values, but they may think it. A 360° assessment is usually completed online by you, your peers and direct reports and is anonymous. Everyone is given the same questions to answer. There are numerous formats for reports available. The one I use is 'Everything DiSC' (dominance, influence, steadiness, conscientiousness). Depending on which assessment you choose there is often a space to write comments. The scores are then calculated and you will receive a report showing how you see yourself compared to how your peers and direct reports see you.

A 360° assessment will help you understand how other people see you as a leader. You will receive a report and discover your greatest strengths and areas for development. If you are serious about being a great leader then I highly recommend it. A 360° assessment will:

- Help raise your self-awareness as a leader

- Improve your leadership effectiveness

- Give you an insight into how other people see you

- Help you to understand your leadership style and behaviours

- Discover what behaviours employees want to see more or less of

- Provide a report with actions and strategies

A coach will then be able to support you as you start to act on the results of the 360° assessment. It's important that you do act on it, otherwise you might be seen as weak by those who contributed. There is no point in doing an assessment if you are not going to take the feedback and make changes.

Communication is critical

Employees want to be communicated with. They want to know what is going on in the business, good and bad. I encourage my clients to set up regular communication channels with their employees. There can never be too much communication. Answering the following questions will help you assess the quality of your communication with your employees.

- What ways are you communicating with your team?

- How often are you communicating with your team? Daily, weekly monthly, annual meetings?

- What do you communicate to them?

- Do you have an agenda?

- Do you discuss financials with employees? Many business owners don't want to discuss numbers; they are frightened to share the numbers.

- Do you talk to people and explain what you really want for your business and from them? If you don't tell them, how are they to know?

- Do you talk about sales, targets and goals?

- Do you put your message across so that everyone understands it? A message is successful only when both the sender and the receiver perceive it in the same way. How are you integrating the values into your communication?

During my interview with Dan Ralphs, Dream Manager at Infusionsoft, he reported that Clate Mask, the CEO, says, 'If the people you lead are not rolling their eyes with the mention of values, you're not talking about them enough.'

This is true. I can't stress enough how much you need to talk about the values and how they must be integrated into everything you do if you want your business to be a success.

Regular communication helps employees stay motivated, lets them know they are valued and encourages them to stay focused on the company purpose and goals. Communication is two-way feedback.

Active listening

Often, as leaders, we talk too much and don't listen enough. You can learn so much from listening to what people have to say. When was the last time you listened to what your staff had to say? I mean *really* listened? Usually, when you are having a conversation with someone, instead of listening to what they are saying you are thinking about what you can say next or how they are wrong, how you could help or how you would do something different. The problem here is that you are not fully listening. You become distracted by your own thoughts and fail to hear what the other person is saying.

Learning to listen actively will help you to retain information. Learn to pause before you speak so you can think about the effect of your words and pay attention for longer. Don't interrupt. Stay focused on what the person is saying and try to shut out any distractions. Show that person you are listening to them by nodding your head and smiling. Active listening is rewarding for the person who is talking to you and makes them feel valued. It can also help reduce misunderstandings.

Many years ago, I coached a senior manager on his listening skills. He was struggling with his relationships with his direct reports and his peers. He lacked the ability to fully listen to people while they had a conversation. He wanted to jump in and solve the problem or ask questions. He was not aware of how this behaviour impacted the individual or the business. His self-awareness was low. How do you feel when you know the person you are talking to is not really listening and can't wait to give you their idea on what you should do?

We worked together to put strategies in place for him to recognise his behaviours and to take responsibility for them. This resulted in improved relationships for him, his peers and direct reports.

Trust

People trust great leaders. If employees don't trust you then you will not get the desired culture or the business results that you are looking for. Employees need to believe in you as a leader. You must build trust. Trust is not something that will happen overnight.

Ways you can start to gain trust as the leader:

- Be consistent in what you do
- Build relationships with people
- Listen to what people have to say
- Deliver results
- Have clarity on what you want to achieve
- Talk to employees
- Walk around the company

A survey by PWC revealed that 50% of chief executives considered a lack of trust to be a major threat to their company growth.[10] Without a good leader the culture will fail. Behaviour change starts at the top.

---

10 *Redefining Business Success in a Changing World*, Annual Global CEO Survey 2016, PWC.

We have now looked at five of the steps in the P.E.O.P.L.E.™ System. Let's move on to Step Six, which is the final step: engagement.

Summary

Building a great culture starts with you, the leader. You need to live the values that you want to see. Employees will be watching your behaviours. As a leader it can be difficult to get feedback on your behaviours and leadership style. To raise your self-awareness and develop your leadership skill, start working with a coach.

Complete a 360° assessment to give you insights into how others see you. When you have the results, work with your coach on an action plan.

Active listening and building trust are important leadership skills. Communicating to your employees is critical, whether it is good or bad news. When you communicate, always link it to the values.

Action steps

- Reflect on your actions and behaviour each day
- List three things where your behaviour demonstrates the values

- In what areas are you not demonstrating the behaviours? Why? What can you do about this?

- Find the right coach for you

- Arrange a 360° assessment

- What is the effect of your leadership style? How do others see you?

- What are you going to do differently moving forward?

- Plan how, when and what you are going to communicate to employees

- Practice active listening

RETAIN

Introducing 'Retain'

As discussed throughout *Recruit, Inspire and Retain*, employees are no longer going to stay with your business forever. They no longer want a job for life. Yet increasing staff turnover can make running a business difficult.

When you employ people, there are things you can actively do to encourage them to stay. Putting these in place will help increase your retention rates:

- Recruit people who are aligned to your values and who believe in your company purpose

- Make employees feel valued

- Encourage employee ownership

- Give employees authority to make decisions

- Let them have a say, value their ideas and opinions

- Live the values

- Be a great leader

- Communicate regularly on what is happening in the business, good or bad

- Reward and give recognition for a job well done
- Give employees opportunities to develop with an understanding that at some stage they will leave
- Have fun and celebrate success

CHAPTER NINE

Engagement

Engagement is the sixth and final step of the P.E.O.P.L.E.™ System. In Chapter Two, I defined culture as 'it's the way we do things round here'. It's the personality of the company, it's what makes you unique. The way I define employee engagement is 'how employees feel things are done around here'.

Employee engagement is not just about having happy employees who enjoy coming to work. Employee engagement improves business outcomes. Highly engaged employees become so involved in their work and go above and beyond what is typically required or expected of them. Highly engaged employees focus on the purpose and values of the business.

'Highly engaged employees make the customer experience. Disengaged employees break it.'

TIMOTHY R. CLARK, founder and CEO of LeaderFactor

Almost everything that happens in the workplace has a direct impact on how employees commit to their work. The environment, the leaders, managers, training and development all play a part in engagement. To retain staff you need to get them engaged.

Why your business needs engaged employees

A lot of research has been conducted around employee engagement. Let's take a look at some of the findings.

- Organisations with highly engaged employees had an average three-year revenue growth 2.3 times greater than companies whose employees were only engaged at an average level[11]

- Disengaged workers had 37% higher absenteeism, 49% more accidents, and 60% more errors and defects[12]

---

11 'Focusing on Employee Engagement: How to Measure it and Improve it', UNC Kenanflager Business School blog (18 June 2015).

12 'Engaging Employees', *Smith Magazine* (Winter 2014), Queens School of Business.

- Teams with high employee engagement rates are 21% more productive[13]

Highly engaged employees become brand ambassadors for your business. They will tell people how great it is to work in your business. This will attract customers and people who will want to come and work for you. They will tell friends and family how great the workplace is and encourage them to apply for jobs.

Engaging employees

Hopefully by now you can see the business benefits of creating a great workplace culture. Not only does the business benefit from this, but the employees benefit too. We spend most of our lives at work and it's important that we enjoy what we do and that we are happy doing it. When we understand the purpose of what we are doing and we feel valued, the results are amazing.

Employees want to feel they are part of something bigger. They want to feel a sense of belonging and know that the contributions they make have an impact.

---

13 'Managing Employee Risk Requires a Culture of Compliance', *Business Journal* (29 March 2016), Gallup.

In an ideal world you want all employees to be engaged, but not all of them will be. In fact, some will struggle with the culture that's being created. That's when you, as the leader, have difficult decisions to make. You may need to say goodbye to these employees. That can be hard, especially if they have worked in the business for a long time, but it's the right thing to do. You need all employees on board, otherwise the People Disease will spread and start to infect all your hard work. It only takes one bad apple. You will live to regret keeping people in the business if they are not engaged or are the wrong culture fit.

Ways to measure culture

This is difficult to do but measures need to be in place and you need to monitor the effectiveness of the culture. Remember, culture is 'how we do things around here'. It's made up of your core values and behaviours. This is what will drive the success of your business.

One way is to measure the behaviours of your employees. The more employees are consistently displaying those behaviours, the more the culture you want to create will grow and become the norm. These can be measured in one-to-one meetings and in annual company surveys. Are the values and behaviours being lived? What evidence do you have?

A great company culture improves customer service.

- Are your customers happier? Are you getting less complaints?

- Has productivity increased?

- Has communication improved in the business?

- Look back at the People Disease issue you had previously

- Are you able to recruit the right people?

- Has sickness absence reduced?

- Is staff turnover lower?

- Is profit up? How is the bottom line affected?

- Do you have a queue of people wanting to come and work for you?

- Is your brand known?

> 'If you are an employer who hasn't experienced an engaged employee who owns their work, then you don't really get it, you don't really understand why having engaged employees is so much better, and so worth the investments in culture. Our sort of mantra around here is "Happy employees equal happy customers, equal happy shareholders." For us, we believe that culture is a strategic advantage in the way

that we think about our business. It is the top priority for all of our leaders. Written down, top priority.'

DAN RALPHS, Dream Manager, Infusionsoft

To be continued...

Culture is critical to your business success. Culture is one of the top priorities for business owners (Deloitte).[14] Culture is no longer being farmed out to HR to implement. HR can be there to support it, but this is for the business owner and leader. Culture change doesn't happen overnight. It takes years and it's a continuous process. It never stops. You can't ever say that the culture is done. It's never done. You have to keep embedding the culture into everything you do. The more you do it, the more it becomes a way of life. It becomes the way we do things around here. Don't try and do it all at once because you won't be able to and it will fail. Focus on one top priority.

Summary

Engagement is not just about having happy employees. Employee engagement has huge benefits to the business.

---

14   Yeo, V and Knott, A, 'Shape Culture. Drive Strategy' (2016), Deloitte.

To get high engagement you need purpose, values, trust, communication, good leadership, development, and for employees to feel valued.

Culture needs to be measured. Culture is an ongoing process, it never ends.

Engaged employees will have a positive impact on your business.

Action steps

Focus on one priority. Identify the area you are going to focus on. Download my P.E.O.P.L.E.™ wheel at www.jacquimann.com/resources.

Next step – complete the exercises:

- Where you are now?
- Where do you want to be?
- What is the number one priority you are going to focus on in your business?
- What and how are you going to measure the culture impact?

Final words

In Chapter One, I talked about what I call 'People Disease' and how I had identified three problems that business owners had, which were causing this disease:

1. You struggle to recruit the right people

2. Employees don't do things the way you want them done

3. Employees are not as passionate about the business as you are

I told you there was no pill to fix it but there was a cure called 'culture'. I then introduced you to the P.E.O.P.L.E.™ System.

By following the steps you will start on your journey of curing your people problems. I hope you can see how each step links back to curing one of the three problems. By implementing the P.E.O.P.L.E.™ System you will:

1. Get everyone aligned to your purpose

2. Attract and retain the right people

3. Boost motivation and staff engagement

4. Create a culture that is unique to your business and becomes an asset

Remember, everyone deserves to have a great place to work. Get engagement right and employees will have as much passion for the business as you do.

At the beginning of the book I said I wanted to start an entrepreneur's cultural revolution. I asked if you would join me. Now you've read the book and can understand the massive impact culture can make on your business I will ask you again. Will you join me in creating an entrepreneur's cultural revolution?

I would love to know how you get on defining and building your culture, so please contact me and share your culture journey.

Join our Entrepreneur's Cultural Revolution group on Facebook: www.facebook.com/groups/entrepreneursculturalrevolution

Acknowledgements

Thank you to all my family, especially my husband Dave, who has encouraged and supported me during the writing of this book. At times I thought it would never be completed.

Without the support of my amazing team at J Mann Associates I would not have been able to take the time away from the business to write this book. Thank you, Janine Toulson, Fiona Screen and Charlene Appleby.

Thank you to Martin Norbury for his constant belief in me and my P.E.O.P.L.E.™ System.

Thanks to the Dent team, especially Daniel Priestley for encouraging me to write a book, and Lucy McCarraher for her expert knowledge and understanding when things got a little tough.

A huge thank you to Kelly Wolske at Zappos and Dan Ralphs at Infusionsoft. I appreciate the time you spent on the phone sharing insights into your company cultures. I would also like to thank you for allowing me to use the information in this book.

To everyone who has given me feedback – I really appreciate you taking the time to read my book and make comments, especially Jacki Norbury, Georgina El Morshdy, and Clive and Julie Bingham.

Thanks also to Pete Cann and Sunny Sandwell for allowing me to share their stories.

The Author

 Jacqui Mann is an HR expert who specialises in creating great places to work. As well as providing HR advice to business owners across the UK, she helps forward-thinking business owners implement the P.E.O.P.L.E.™ System.

Jacqui has studied the wide-reaching impact people make on an organisation for over twenty years. She's seen first-hand the difference the right culture and environment can make to a company's results. Company culture and change management are her speciality. She has worked with both public and private sector companies, supporting them with culture change programmes.

She trained with the Tavistock Consultancy on Organisational Development and Change. She is a Chartered Member of the CIPD, a member of the British Psychological Society and a certified DiSC trainer.

She is also a qualified business coach and a Graduate of the Institute of Master Coaches, and has coached business owners and Fortune 500 company leaders and their teams. Her passion is in supporting SMEs to create and define great workplace cultures. She runs regular workshops and speaks about company culture at conferences and events.

You can contact Jacqui via
her websites or on social media:

www.jacquimann.com

www.jmassociates.org

www.linkedin.com/in/jacquimann

www.facebook.com/jacquimannhrexpert

www.twitter.com/jacqui_mann